GRAY MIST AT DAWN

The Story of Kriya Yoga's Hidden Master – Sri Shellji

By

Steven Cozzi

ISBN: 1-4033-8891-1 (e-book)
ISBN: 1-4033-8892-X (Paperback)

This book is printed on acid free paper.

COVER CONCEPT DESIGN – Anthony K. Cozzi

1stBooks - rev. 12/04/02

DEDICATION

To my wise and loving benefactor Sri Shellji for revealing, lightening and clearing the path for me. To Marjorie and Deborah, his first and second wives for their continued loving-kindness. Also to Paramahansa Yogananda, Babaji, Mataji and all the Kriya Masters for their silent and steadfast guidance, which has kindled my Liberation. Finally to the Transfinite Masters, Ultraterrestials, Angels and all "Unselfish Service to Other" beings whose invisible hands helped shape my life.

And the LORD spoke to his children through the lips of Chacti, saying: "In the course of your "becoming" you have disposed of your kingdom that was my crown, and of your freedom that was my spirit, and your Grace that was my blood. Now it is spilled into the Earth where lies my heart, and through the veins of lighted stars, so it shall once again feed my brain, and stay the hunger of my eyes. For, as you now are no longer the cells of my body, but the chain of the Earth, yet my children shall not forever dwell in the earth, they shall "race upon starlight," pushing back into my flesh, as a child struggling to reenter the womb, and there it is said that the time of man will close."

From the 30 million year old "Book of Ii" from the land now under the Pacific, Mu or Eden, translated by Maia+ Christine Nartoomid – Copyright 1978 – www.spiritmythos.org

Special thanks to Linda M. DiNoto, M.A. for editing

INTRODUCTION

Many times I have pondered on how I might convey the sacred wisdom that I received from the heart and mind of my benefactor Shelly Trimmer. I, realize that the transmission of this teaching is now in the past/present. An important future/past task looms before me. How to present the written dissemination of this knowledge?

The experience of telling a special, but personal, story and then seeing the confused or blank look on the other person's face is, I believe, quite common. What is usually said is: "I guess you had to have been there". This is my challenge: "To somehow bring you there." Every writer is confronted with trying to recreate an experience real or imagined. In this situation the descriptions are complicated by the fact that we have multi-dimensional presentations that comprise a collation of thoughts, feelings and symbols happening in the present, past and future!

With that being said, the experiences contained in these pages encompass a rare variety of transcendental messages. Being oral teachings, these utterances will of course suffer the limitations of language; yet I feel they will retain their transformational tone. They are only words if you choose to look at them in such a way. Yet from time immemorial, mystical teachers have attempted to convey a deeper and hidden meaning that always seems to remain within the symbols and between the lines.

I have striven to bring forth these teachings in their unadulterated and original format. However, certain poetic license and grammatical alterations were necessary. For example, certain sections of information needed to be put into a more understandable chronological order. I have endeavored to keep all alterations to a minimum.

I had the extreme good karma to be able to visit with Shelly twenty-two times over a period of twenty-seven and a half years, (from 1969 to 1996). My visits were as short as one hour and as long as nine days. About 60% of my time with him was recorded. These recordings comprise well over 150 hours of audio archives. About 100 of those most important hours have been transcribed for these volumes. The very best of these conversations are contained within this volume.

Shelly had a unique and unconventional form of communication. He often said his manner of speaking was a form that was mathematical in its expression. I can concur, and add that his mind was filled with the most abstract concepts imaginable. As best as we can figure, he often thought in German, while using internal symbols from Hebrew, Chinese, Sanskrit and a few angelic/magical/ mathematical languages. Given his propensity for seemingly unrelated abstract statements, it all had to come out as conversational English at some point!

Toward the end of his earthly stay he called himself the "Answer Guru." He would say; "Remember, it's the type of question and the way you phrase it. That's the secret in getting the desired answer. I have more answers then I realize. I also need to know these answers." I can only hope that I asked as many of the important questions as possible. I do know one thing, I never ran out of questions, nor did he ever tire in answering them.

Mystery after mystery unfolded before me in an endless panorama of directions, possibilities, and discoveries. It wasn't possible or necessary for him to explain them all in detail, but with most of the greater teachings many excellent clues were given. They have served as needed advice when dealing with subtle strategies of the path.

I recall him saying that information was one of freest things in this world, but that the type of information that he was really interested in did not always come from this earth.

So dear reader, if, it happens that you are interested in a fancy new "marketing technique" for spiritual growth, or maybe a "franchise Guru" near you, or possibly a "we got all the answers, nobody in heaven but us" kind of attitude, then you should continue your search because that stuff is NOT here in this book. Shelly and the lineage of Kriya Yogis have always been, and will continue to be interested only in the quality element within teachers and students. In the final analysis quantity has very little meaning.

That being said, this is the information he gave me while on earth. It is for you to pick and choose in the harvest of ideas and simple truths herein presented. Some information you may find digestible, while certain concepts may go to seed, only to sprout within your future memories. It is my sincere wish that this book will cause you to reflect on the concepts outlined in the following pages, and that your spirit will profit immensely from doing so.

TABLE OF CONTENTS

CHAPTER 1.

BODISATTVA IDEAL

It was autumn, and the sounds were different now. There was a covering and a revealing of sounds. It was the leaves; they were the ones that caused it all. They masked the many sounds with their wind driven noise. They also showed the movement of things: birds, squirrels, rabbits, dogs, cats; all could be heard, and then seen. Under the clear skies of October, they were seen.

The refreshing coolness was vividly present. Nature was slowly and perceptibly in a mild slumber, not yet in its deep sleep of winter. It was an in-between time, a time filled with moments of light and shadow. The bounty of summer and harvest of fall somehow gave a balance to things. People were happy but it was a different happy, a strange happy, a happy they had come to accept.

It was an in-between time and almost everyone knew it. They knew it like they had always known things, not from books or gossip, but from somewhere inside. Maybe it was the light on the leaves that created this quiet place, a still place of knowing. They all held these ideas in their minds, but rarely did they share. What was the point? It was so obvious.

Then there was the need to be careful, and it was something you learned early on. Careful without fear, but non-the-less cautious about what you said. People knew things here, a great many things, things that people in Cleveland or Buffalo did not know existed.

It was the natural magic of this season, and it reflected something hidden, something strange and different. After all, that's what was important, because the unusual was elevated here, and the common was just accepted. That unusual stuff, that is what made you think, that's what made the feelings turn into questions. Well, there were always those undercurrents, the eddies of rich feelings, and the oddity of certain emotions.

Many of these knowing perceptions were contained in the simple movements of the eyes. It could at times unnerve you and make you uncomfortable. You had to get used to it, but everyone knew you could never really get used to it. As the years passed, you developed a strategy to deal with it, and that "it" was energy. It had to be energy, just look at all the things that have happened. They all heard the stories and they remembered them. They were not the stories you could really forget. Sometimes for mental comfort they would pretend to forget. On the surface of things it seemed like a typical American town. Was it an average town, with average problems?

Every town has its disputes, conflicts and differing points of view. The legal system handled some of these and the churches take a portion of the others. Many disputes in this part of the state were still handled in the old fashioned way, simply by talking it out and finding some way of mutual compromise. A man's word and handshake meant something. Of course, all this was what a superficial observer might see. Limited in scope, they really didn't see the whole picture. Oh their eyes may have worked fine, but that's not the type of seeing that some of the people used.

The psychic light energy was read and it was used in a variety of ways. Not everyone was adept in doing it, yet most would acknowledge that it was the basis of many unusual and extraordinary occurrences. It could heal and it could hurt. No matter what went on it was used to solve problems and you prayed to God that you were not on the receiving end of its malicious intent. Some folks had an abundance of it, and others very little. Certain people used it wisely, and others, those nasty, spiteful, revengeful "others," did not. You could stand clear from them, or be courteous or even play stupid. Yet it was actually quite difficult to ignore all the on-going dramas and their accompanying phenomena.

This region of Pennsylvania where he was born was called the Dutch Country; it extended from Erie in the north, to the south central part of the state. Deutch (meaning German) was the actual word, but since WWI the phrase "Pennsylvania Dutch Country" was most often used. German immigrants had been arriving there for over 75 years. They carried with them few belongings. The most important item that they had in their possession was a point of view, an attitude stemming from an old and proven way of life. Most called it the ancient way of their forefathers, but everyone knew it was pagan. You didn't say the word, but you knew it was the primal, potent and proven way. They came from all parts of Europe but mostly Germany. They all had their country tales, folk medicine and an ardent belief that true spirituality always trumps organized religion. Sure they called themselves Christian, and many went to church, but there also was a private side to this community. There, the deeper meanings of life were expressed in contemporary stories that started and ended with whispers and glances.

History had shown that the Roman legions and the armies of the great Ghengis Khan did not kill their ideas. The Church of Rome with its inquisition and the radical intensity of the Protestant revolution didn't stop it either. Nothing really could stop this tribal wisdom, this inspired geomancy of life.

In this part of America the clash of cultures was somewhat lessened. There was a real common bond that developed between some of the immigrants and the indigenous peoples. Earth magic, pagan beliefs and a naturalistic philosophy united a small group within each camp. This unique, cooperative sharing resulted in the techniques of what has been called "Pow Wow Magic". It was the distilled wisdom from two continents and it really worked well for both cultures.

*   *   *

It was the fall of 1921, and soon he (Shelly) would have a birthday, his fourth. He liked his birthday time because it was close to All Hallows Eve. It was a strange time in an even stranger place. A time when the various dramas of the past year were acted out. You got the definite impression that some of the acting and customs were not really flights of fantasy as much as expressions of something real, something sublime, but terribly real.

He knew his life was different. He was very aware that his parents and others did not necessarily share his perceptions of certain events.

Early on, he had noticed that everyone heard sounds that came out of the mouth. After all, you could see the lips move and it was clear that there were the deeper father tones and the higher mother tones.

He also heard the other sounds, the sounds that were words, but in this case the lips didn't have to move. It was really amusing to watch people using words and thinking thoughts. The difficulty was that he heard them both! People didn't say what they were thinking, and not only that, they often said the opposite. It was confusing, as well as being disappointing. They thought one thing but said another, and sometimes did things different from the first two. No wonder the people of this world have big problems, he thought. There is something wrong with them, and it's not right.

He knew that one of the major difficulties was those containers: the shells or compartments that people called bodies. He tried so hard to get used to that fact; it wasn't easy. It was not like this before, he thought. It was not so difficult in the other places, the many, many, other places he had visited. This was a challenge and it was a very difficult adjustment to make. It was definitely confining this body he had. It had to be fed, washed, and one third of the day it had to rest. It was a limiting circumstance and a permanent one for now. Somehow he would have to deal with it, and he knew it was a 24-hour a day job.

Then there were the interactions with his parents. This was another complex issue, and like the rest of his life, nowhere near the so-called normal. The intellectual division between his parents was obvious. His father had a photographic memory for numbers and a strong scientific aptitude. However, he never capitalized on these strengths. Instead he worked in an ice cream factory.

His mother was a different type of person. She did not have a developed intellect, but, her intuition was very reliable and her psychic abilities pronounced. She also had a striking physical and spiritual beauty that radiated from her. Her pleasant and concerned countenance imbued a feeling of confidence within him. He also liked hearing his mother's voice and her thoughts. She was caring, nurturing and very protective toward him and others.

His father, well that was a difficult story. He had a hidden resentment, and at times a cruelty that was undeniable. Oh sure, he would brag about his son at times, saying how smart he was, yet never coming to the obvious. "This boy is exceedingly smarter then I am". This didn't stop him from stepping right up to gloat about the praise that others bestowed on his child.

He remembered well the prophecies that foretold of his son's birth. The rumors and utterances were well known among the people who had the gift. The gift that they wisely used, and for some the gift they chose to abuse. They talked about a highly advanced soul, a leader, and one whose military abilities were unmatched. He's going to be a great general; the seers would say. They had divined it in dreams, and through various signs, and they knew it would happen.

During the last minutes of the birthing hour his father remembered the watches, those fine timepieces that were set to the reliable railroad time. He and the boy's grandfather both kept a vigil at the bedroom door, and at the first cry they recorded the time. It had to be correct so that the casting of the horoscope would be accurate, then life's events could be timed with precision.

He seemed like a normal baby, crying and red, with eyes mostly closed. His mother and the midwife knew differently. They had seen them; they had noticed them right away. It made them both wonder: are they a blessing or a curse? Were they some sort of strange sense of humor or a hidden omen? It was the ears of the baby. They were the average size, but both of them came to a very distinct point! It was odd, alien, and enough of a curiosity to create ridicule.

His mother had to remedy this. She must do something. Keeping his head covered was a temporary solution, but as he grew she employed another. The family, neighbors and friends all wanted to see him and they would talk. They would talk about her baby, her strange and beautiful baby. She began to rub the pointed tops of his ears. Sometimes they would bleed from the rubbing, then she would let them heal before she started again. His mother repeated this process many times with determination and with love. The stories about his ears subsided, but the other stories about him never did.

Then they started to come, the visitors. They came to see him and to speak to him. They were family, extended family and friends of both. It wasn't everyday, but it was consistent. It started just before he was three and it lasted till he was about seven. His mother knew why they came. They were polite but they always asked for the same thing.

They wanted a few private moments with him, five minutes or more was usually enough. It was her darling boy child they wanted to speak with, but she knew all too well that it was much more then that.

It was partly ritual, and a little worship but mostly deeper psychological needs that brought them. They all needed to confess, to verbalize their real and imagined sins, their mistakes and problems. They spoke of thoughts and deeds that they kept hidden. It was a wonderful feeling of release when they were done. They really felt better on the inside, and they knew that now they, at least, had a chance to be forgiven. The sharing of secrets and the upliftment they felt afterwards, that is what it was all about, and that's what brought them back again.

His mother and father asked him to listen, and his own curiosity inspired him to hear their words. In the beginning of this process he didn't understand what they were saying. He understood the words but often the meaning was clouded with emotion and innuendo. He soon found out that, the majority of what they felt was sin, had to do with sex. Many felt that something about the act itself raised doubt. They felt that the primal emotions that drove them were at times beyond their control. Then they also had to deal with the overwhelming ecstatic feelings of the act itself. The lying and betrayal that became part of the process was the real problem, yet most seemed unconcerned with this area. Many of the words rode on torrents of emotion. They found the whole sexual drama to be a powerful and scary occurrence, and to the confessors this meant that it probably was wrong and sinful.

He didn't say hardly a word; he just looked into their eyes, nodded and occasionally smiled. It was obvious that they felt relieved and calmed by the visits. He knew he was doing something good for them and he learned from each visit. He was beginning to see what made humans tick and it was disturbing. It was clear to him that their minds were undisciplined and prone to a variety of emotional compulsions. He was beginning to see that there were the ordinary problems and behaviors and the other extraordinary ones. This second group he felt was the one that he understood more. He could see that most people played their various roles and acted in certain ways, yet, behind it all he noticed that a few were more conscious of their actions. They were the ones that went through the motions as if life were a game to be played without losing themselves in the drama. They were the ones that had the gift; the gift of seeing and knowing. It most often came through the parents, where one or both had received it from their parents. Although he had just started to study science, he did realize that spiritual tendencies were intimately connected to genetic inheritance.

During this period he had one memorable and frightening visit from an uncle who confessed to him about an affair he was having. When he finished he took a handgun out of his coat and put the barrel into his stomach. He told him that if he ever revealed what he had said, he would kill him. There was more fear in his uncle then in himself. Now he knew what some humans were capable of doing. Unfortunately, it was only the beginning of a life where he would encounter ruthlessness and violence, sometimes at an unprecedented level.

He was a child who loved books, but his education was also richly supplemented by his keen observational abilities. Quite often he would crawl out of bed at night and put his ear at the crack of the bedroom door. He was then able to hear his parents talk, and if they had guests, then this was an added bonus. It was more informative and entertaining then radio and most books. What he heard was the most interesting rumors and events, the ones that were really significant in the community. In was truly a local report on the paranormal occurrences that were taking place under the pretence of an apparently not-so-normal town and region. It was great fun and exciting. He found the stories to be very insightful as well as stimulating to his imagination.

He always felt that his mother knew he was listening, somehow she could feel him. After all she had seen his other body, the light double many times. His spirit/dream body was very active, and she readily accepted it as an attribute of an exceptional child. Anyway, he was determined to get the information he needed both from this world and the other.

His physical growth was a slow process and it was obvious he would be on the short side in height. He had a delicate built and clear radiant skin. He preferred vegetables, cheese, fruit and bread. He had

7

to be careful how much he ate because he would, on occasion, get pains in the upper intestinal area. Later on in life he would discover that he had three kidneys. The third one was semi-dormant and it pressed against his upper intestinal area.

He soon learned that the local witches had wars when the normal ways of settling disputes was found to be inadequate, or just because their spiteful nature caused them to do it anyway. He also learned that many times there was no logical or proper way to reconcile the variety of differences that arose. At the basis of these problems were the usual things: sex, power, and money.

Everyone knew who the witches were and each one had her temporary or somewhat permanent allies. There the general magic that many knew, and then there was the magic that was specific to families or individuals. Spirits were summonsed, natural forces were employed and spells were cast. He could hear all about it at least two or three nights a week, at his bedroom door. Being a little Scorpio Sun Sign, he loved the secrets he discovered, and he had carefully hidden their precious lessons deep within his memory.

School was another matter entirely. It was "ok to boring" in the early grades, but as time went on, he began to openly question his teachers. His spontaneous aptitude for debate was usually not accepted. This was why the visitors stopped coming, as his intense individuality set in more and more. Mentally and spiritually, he past quickly from a very young child, to a boy, who was really a young man.

His father's cruelty came and went, and it was obvious that he was the first of many opponents he would have to deal with in this life. His father could not deal with his significant presence and all the subtle yet powerful feelings it evoked. The strategy of interacting with his son made him realize that he had to deal with a level of intelligence that was beyond what he had thought possible. Living in the same house with such a child meant that he had to be careful of what he said and did.

The oddity was that there was very little real dialog between his son and he, especially when it came to his behavior. There really didn't have to be, he could feel that the child knew his tendencies, and further that he didn't like many of them. "This boy has such a probing way of looking at me," he thought. "He knows all my secrets and imperfections and he expects me to try and improve." Well, I am the father, and I will deem what is right and wrong," he grimaced.

All of this war of wills brought out his father's sadistic side. When the boy was still quite young, he would tie him up and beat him on his bare feet. When he had grown older he forced him into very hard labor around the house. He had him lift so many bags of coal that his intervertebral discs had been severely damaged before he was twelve.

The child's opposing reactions were always caught in crossfire of emotions. There was his protective concern for his mother and younger sister. He wanted to keep them out of harm's way by engaging the tyrannical moods of his father by himself. What little respect he had for his father evaporated early on, as a mature boy painfully learned what his father was capable of doing. Years later there was a very overdue and decisive confrontation which settled matters.

His younger sister was somewhat of another matter. Although she respected him as an older brother, he noticed that she had an unusual psychic energy field. He loved her, but because of this fact he had to deal with her in special way.

There was certainly a plethora of suspenseful dramas that seemed to fill his life. So, quite naturally, he viewed life as a complex series of mysterious events. He was also keenly aware that a certain power was what made things happen. The power of whom, and the power to do what, that was the real question. He loved science but he realized that it only had part of the answers that he sought. Life had revealed to him that the magic of spirit had the highest knowledge. This was the knowledge that he so ardently longed for, in his dreams, and during all his waking hours.

"The child is father of the man"
—William Wordsworth

CHAPTER 2.

INITIATION

The plane was beginning to descend and so was I. It had made a slow turn west and so had I, and it was near its destination and I was too. It was really only the beginning of another journey, which was contained within many journeys. It was a voyage into some unknown something. Some strange and yet comfortable place. It was a curve in time and space that would forever change my destiny.

The "brand new" and innocent excitement was there. It was like the first day of summer vacation, the new bike on Christmas morning, a spring day in the forest. The anticipation had all of these wonderful feelings and something deeper, an unfathomable awareness of entering a new world.

The turquoise water was made clearer by the white sand beaches. It was March 1969, and a series of fortunate events were now culminating. I could only wonder how this amazingly good piece of karma had somehow opened a new door for me. The nature of the trip was filled with a certain mystical synchronicity. My seeking, I felt, had finally placed me in an uncommon awareness field that was dedicated to growth.

There was palm trees and jungle on both sides of the runway and there were no jet ways protruding from the terminal. The moveable stairway came up to the plane's door. The heat of the Sun and the warm moist air enveloped me at the same time. I started to walk the 50 yards or so to the terminal, when a woman seemed to stand out. She was middle aged and she looked to me like a librarian, and a Sunday school teacher as well. Our eyes locked in on each other and I continued to walk toward her.

Her face beckoned me to approach her and the kindness that poured forth from her was quite magnetic.

"You are Steve Cozzi," she said in a certain voice.

"Yes," I said and we both smiled on cue.

"I'm Marjorie, and I am Shelly's wife". We both turned toward the terminal. "My car is this way," she said.

"Let me get my bag and we can go," I answered.

The car was a 1952 Buick. It was old but well cared for, it had a lot of chrome and it held to the road like a tank with wheels. There was mostly jungle on both sides of the road and I had the impression that she had taken the back scenic road. We exchanged some pleasantries, but I was apprehensive to go even a small step further.

I could feel that she was reading me like a book. Every little body movement and each nuance of tone in my speech was intuitively recorded and analyzed. She was playing with me in some unknown and remote sort of way. It was like there was some sort of experiment going on and I was the subject.

There wasn't anything phony or pretentious about her speech or actions.

However, she did create an air of expectation, an anticipation of something that was definitely unexpected by me. It was pure fun to her, like some kind of spontaneous ritual; or maybe a hidden surprise that she seemed to guard so carefully. Somehow, I felt that she was playfully pretending to be whom she was. It really wasn't that noticeable, yet she was allowing me to see this for some reason.

The drive was less then 5 miles and we turned down a shaded street that was still more country then city. We approached a modest, small white house that was more of a vacation cottage then anything else. Two enormous oak trees stood near it. One of them was on the south side and the other near the street to the east, thus completely shading the house. The Florida smell was strong here. It was a mild rotting smell combined with a fresh foliage smell and a wisp of sail air for seasoning. We entered from a rear storeroom; it had a workshop bench but the room was surprisingly uncluttered with things. We walked through a very simple and small kitchen and dinning room combination.

She then turned right and motioned, while saying, "This is your room." It was small but the bed looked decent and I could smell something exotic that was growing outside the window. I thought I was finally here, or home, or someplace that had deep meaning. An intense feeling of joy welled up within me. I laid down on the bed not realizing that I was in a altered state of awareness. I think I must have slept maybe an hour.

I awoke with a similar awareness of deep stillness that I was only semi-conscious of when I fell asleep. It was quieter now, a deeper calm seemed to be overlaid upon what was normal. It was a strange hush, contained within the common absence of noise that was now more familiar, because of the profound feeling of quiet that it was part of.

There seemed to be some muffled noises coming from the kitchen. I slowly got up not really noticing that my actions were quite slow. I left the room and walked in a cautious manner toward the living room.

I didn't want to ignore Majorie in the kitchen, so I said a quick "Hi." She casually gave me a brief look as if she wanted to say something.

"Why say hi when we both know that you are up and walking to the living room," was the mental message I got.

"O.K., O.K.," I thought. I don't have to be overly friendly when she obviously knows what I am doing anyway. Would she know what I was doing without seeing me?" Back in my hippy days I would have thought that she was high and maybe a natural high at that. It wasn't really appropriate to say anything in the present circumstances. It's just that I didn't know many people over fifty that had her type of clear awareness.

The living room was a comfortable size and I could see that it opened to a screen porch in front of the house. There was a couch on the south wall with one of three fish tanks to the side of it. The other two fish tanks were opposite of the couch, with a chair on either side of them. The T.V. was in the front of the room on an angle from the couch. I surmised that Shelly must sit on the couch somewhere. I had not noticed it before but the house had a faint smell of tobacco. Shelly smoked? My mind took a skeptical turn. Why should a holy man smoke? Did this mean he took drugs too? No he couldn't be into that. After all, he had meditated for so many years. He was with Yogananda for over three years.

Marjorie's voice interrupted my thoughts. "We will go and pick up Shelly from work in about an hour," she remarked. I got that tingle in my stomach but a slight pressure in my heart offset it. Non-the-less my adrenaline started to fire.

At that very moment Marjorie said, "You can go for a walk if you want."

I think I was out the door in less then two seconds. She wanted to get rid of my nervous energy. It must have been very obvious, but I'm not sure how. I think that I walked around the block in just a little over five minutes, but to me it seemed to go in slow motion. When I walked in she had an odd look on her face.

"Back so soon"? she said. I also heard, "Why is he back so soon?"

I realized that I had almost run around the block. I left without a word and this time I walked slowly.

We both got into the Buick and I remembed I didn't have enough manners to open her door. I was buoyant but still nervous. I simultaneously felt like I was getting on a roller coaster, getting an exam back, and being really high in a very different place. Like maybe in a graveyard, or in a traffic jam, or with my relatives. Then I corrected myself; no it really wasn't like any of those places. Why was I thinking like this anyway? My mind was racing on one level, and peaceful on another.

It was less then a year since I had given up all drugs. That's why I was thinking about what being high was then, and what is was now. I was presently in a different state, but it was so functional, I had to keep analyzing it over and over. We were in a car moving down a road, but I wasn't meditating, nor was I dreaming, but it seemed so much like it. That's what was confusing. I wanted to accept it as normal, and maybe I would at some point. Time was definitely something that I was moving in and out of, so what time was I really talking about? They say perception IS reality, but back then many of my perceptions, concepts, and habits were radically changing. Changing so fast I found myself doing a number of mental reality checks.

We had driven past downtown Bradenton and we were now on the bridge to Palmetto. We passed one light and made a left, then a quick right behind a T.V. repair shop.

"Shelly is a T.V. repairman?" I asked.

"Yes" Majorie said with a very slight chuckle.

I just didn't realize that he had to earn a living, somehow. Didn't anyone give him donations? I thought, "Doesn't he do astrology readings? Why does he have to work in this conventional shop"?

I sat motionless in the car for a few seconds until Marjorie said, "You can come in, you know."

We entered a room where various televisions were lined up on counters. I saw a man short in stature looking into the back of a TV. I could see from the back that his almost completely gray hair was braided in two strands and tucked down into his black sweater. It appeared that his hair went all the way to his waist. I thought, "All that hair and he's an old guy; this is really different."

Marjorie walked over to him and at the same time I took a few steps closer. When he turned around I got shocked, stunned and elated, all in the same instant. His eyes were the largest and most penetrating I had ever seen. I hadn't noticed before hand, but he was wearing thick bifocals for the close up work. The effect and the affect were quite sensational.

"Hi Steve," he said in a voice that was so wonderfully friendly and knowing. I don't really remember if I said hello or just stood there quietly and stared.

Shelly drove on the way home and I sat in back like a little kid they were taking somewhere. I really felt good to be that little kid again. It was a warm and protected feeling. In reality I was a student, and very soon now I would learn what it meant to be a student of Shelly. I realized right then, that in many important areas I was uninformed, somewhat immature and presently quite ignorant. My ego could not stand the idea, but it was true. It was only six months ago that I had read my first book, at the age of twenty-three.

Shelly's eyesight was not the best so he drove very slow between 25 and 30 MPH.

I thought back to when I was a wild teenager and we used to sound the horn and yell at old people driving on the highway. A tingle of guilt welled up in me.

It was all small talk between them both on the way home. However, I did notice that during the conversation they would answer each other without one of them questioning first. I never heard the question! It was amazing; they were having a half audible and telepathic conversation about everyday stuff. It all seemed perfectly normal. Shelly turned the old Buick into the drive way and parked half way under the oak tree on the side of the house.

"The dog would like its walk," Marjorie said.

"Dog, what dog I thought." Well it was a little black longhaired Skipper Key that came up to Shelly.

"How are you little girl," he said.

The dog seemed very happy to see him.

"O.K., we will go out," he said.

We went out the front door and the dog gently pulled Shelly to the side of the house where she was busy sniffing out something.

Shelly turned toward me. "You know a dog can catalog over 250 different smells. She is always trying to find new smells, just like all life forms, they try and extend the limits of what they know. I presume that is why you are here?"

"Yes," I said.

After a few quiet nervous moments, he said, "Let's go in and have dinner."

We sat down at the table, and again I felt like the resident child.

"Shelly is having vegetarian beans and stewed vegetables, is that OK?" Marjorie said. I was about to say yes when she addressed Shelly and asked, "Do you want jam?"

"Yes, beautiful" he said.

"Beautiful?"

"What's this beautiful stuff?" I thought. He never called her by her name, as it turned out. It was always "beautiful" said with a variety of inflections and tones.

While eating I had a chance to observe how Shelly was dressed. He was almost all in black, starting with his engineer boots, simple black pants, a long sleeved black sweater and a long white silk scarf. He wore the silk scarf under the sweater and it resembled an ascot. The scarf covered the central portion of his chest under the sweater. Later I found out that this was his daily attire, and I do mean daily, he never wore anything else! He had about three sets of each, except the shoes, and he just washed and rotated them. It didn't matter whether it was hot or cold, or for any occasion really, the cloths remained the same. (My guess is that he wore this mystical garb for at least forty years or more).

Towards the end of the meal Marjorie made an open comment: "Look how he eats everything on his plate like a good boy."

She said it in a humorous yet mocking way, and it seemed to call forth a response in me. I did not respond. I didn't want to, because I realized it had irritated me. "Does she think I am a little boy, and why is she playing with me?" I was quiet during most of the meal. I just listened to them talk about simple daily affairs. Toward the end I did manage a question.

"Shelly, did you ever eat meat?" He looked at me in a very relaxed way and said, "Yes I had a pork chop once when I was 13 and I didn't like it very much" was his reply.

It was somehow evident in the tone of his voice that it was the only time he had knowingly eaten meat. I was, of course, very impressed with this fact, not realizing that it was taste plus necessity that made him a vegetarian.

After dinner we both migrated to the living room. Shelly sat at the end of the couch. The dog followed as if attached somehow, she snuggled up right next to him. He reached over and took an unfiltered cigarette out of the Pall Mall pack; in a split second it was lit. He took a deep drag followed by a shallow inhale while letting most of the smoke out of his nose exhaling. The cigarette was in his right hand, and when it was free it was gently stroking the dog.

His talking and the ever-present smoking and stroking became an enduring pattern in those early years. The smoke had stained the upper part of his long beard. It made his black and gray beard look blond, at least around the mustache and chin area. His beard was mostly white with small ribbons of darker hair. (He quit smoking in 1976).

I had no beard at the time, but it made me think of when I was hippie and I remembered my mother calling me Rabbi because my beard was quite long. Now I could see that the word Rabbi was totally appropriate for the present situation.

I started talking first, which was the wrong thing to do. I told him that I was in the Air Force and then I was a hippie for a couple of years. In August of 1968 I met his student/disciple Swami Kriyananda (of Chicago, NOT California or India) at his new temple. He listened quietly, but I got the distinct impression that he already knew all of what I was saying.

When he began to speak I realized that there was something powerfully hypnotic about his voice. It was his teaching voice and one that very few could forget. It had a deep male pitch to it, with a cadence that was remarkably consistent and rhythmic. It really was something to listen to because it was somehow mildly disturbing yet soothing at the same time. It made me feel awake yet I could have easily fallen asleep at any moment.

I was at that time so completely happy that I was beside myself, figuratively and literally.

"I knew you had taken LSD, I could tell by your voice," he said.

I must have had a questioning look on my face.

He continued, "There's a certain pitch that I can hear in your voice," he said.

"What does it sound like?" I asked naively.

"It sounds rather moronic," he said bluntly.

This was not the answer I was looking for. After all, LSD was a big part of my awakening. It had helped me see a part of a new world.

"Well, I only took it about 15 times," I said.

"That's enough to affect your cervical center," was his answer.

"OK", I thought, as I quickly stated," I never had a bad trip."

"Well that's good," he said in a voice that seemingly didn't care at that point.

Now I was puzzled, but undeterred, I boldly stated: "Getting high had its moments." I can remember the great bands playing, and the strobe lights flashing and all the beautiful people (as they were called then) were dancing together as one. I found it to be an amazing experience."

"I find it sickening," he interjected.

I immediately told my mind, "Shut up!"

"I tried to go to one of those love-ins," he said. When I got within a block or so, the music was so loud I could feel the various spaces in my intestinal tract between the digesting foods! It was so disturbing I had to turn around and leave," he said.

I was lost for words, and it wouldn't do any good being defensive either, I thought.

After about a half-minute pause he lit another cigarette. I don't know how he did it, but it seemed that the smoke never came my way. Not only that, it had an odd, yet vaguely pleasant smell to it, like someone's homemade incense.

He looked toward me.

"This world, this reality, your reality is not what you think it is," he said.

"Yes," I confidently said.

I knew there were other states of awareness and different realities. Shortly, and in an unsuspecting way I was to find out that I was totally ignorant and completely unprepared to deal with these vast realities of life.

*   *   *

(Shelly wanted to cover a lot of bases on that first visit, but unfortunately I was not ready to grasp most of the concepts. There seemed to be a lot of lost time. I do remember many stories, and no matter what he was talking about, he always managed to come back to those shocking stories. The first visit was not taped, however over the years he repeated almost all of the stories at least once, so they will be covered throughout this volume.

These stories of the first visits were the most incredible collection of the unexplained, macabre, bizarre and unusual events that anyone could possibly imagine. All of them were of the supernatural. Many were directly related to him, but most he collected from a great variety of sources. They were scary and informative, revolting and inspiring, and always shocking, yet insightful. The process was specifically designed to shatter, alter and completely change my concept of reality. The only conclusion I could come to, was, that life was becoming a wonderful, spontaneous and unfathomable mystery yet to be explored.

It didn't matter what he was talking about, my awareness didn't seem to be there completely. I knew that I knew what he was saying; at the very moment I heard his words. I could recite them exactly within an hour of hearing them, but much to my frustration they did not stay in my memory. I always remained very attentive to what he was talking about. Yet it all seemed to enter a place of higher memory, inaccessible in the present. I often wonder if they both left me in the living room staring at the wall in a trance while they had a cup of tea in the kitchen. Shelly was the epitome of politeness, so he wouldn't just leave the room. However, I am quite sure that there were times when he stopped talking for up to 15 minutes. At such times I stared into space in a futile attempt at understanding. This amused him to no end.)

It was dark now and the fish tank lights gave off an eerie aquatic glow. He began to speak again.

"The way to greater Self Conscious Awareness (SCA) is through meditation. The problem is that most people approach it in the wrong way. They sit down to practice it with all kinds of ideas that are incorrect."

"Look, he said, meditation is to be enjoyed! They forget that it's to be enjoyed, so once the astrological aspects that inclined them to experiment with meditation end they then stop doing it. It could be weeks or months, but they stop. Then some start again but very often they will stop yet again."

"You can't force anything in meditation," He continued, "It's not done to atone for sins, or to punish one's Self. It's also not done to prove to yourself how saintly and pious you are. It has to be an enjoyable, daily habit, so how can we do this, he said?"

I had an idea of what he would say next, but as usual my thinking was off the mark.

"You have to slowly build an enjoyable habit," he said in his rhythmic speech. "You start by meditating, only a few minutes, maybe just five minutes. Even though it's the greatest tool we in this life have, you should approach in a relaxed even causal way. Just sit there for five minutes and watch the breath. It's too short of a time for you to feel restless. There are all kinds of emotions that will interfere, but in just a few minutes of time, they really can't interfere that much. You can sit on the floor or in a chair but keep the spine straight, stomach muscles slightly in. Then simply focus on the third eye just above and between the eyebrows".

I had learned Kriya meditation at the Chicago Temple, but I had to admit that his suggestion of "building enjoyment" was the missing ingredient.

"There are just too many thoughts and emotions at play, and if you start to battle with them, you'll get nowhere."

*   *   *

(I remembered the old East Indian Yogi story I had heard: It was the story of the impulsively curious disciple. He had heard his Guru say that there is a most secret mantra, which would evoke a wish-granting demon. The disciple begged and pleaded with Guru to give him the mantra, but out of deep concern, the Guru always said no.

Then one day the Guru realized that there was no way around it, the disciple had to learn a great but dangerous lesson.

The disciple in solitude proceeded to chant the mantra with much excitement and anticipation.

Very soon a powerful demon appeared, and in a deep and echoing voice he said, "Give me work or I will devourer you."

The disciple said, "Build me a great castle," and behold a beautiful castle appeared.

Immediately the demon bellowed, "Give me work or I will devour you."

"Well then fill it with precious stone and metals," and woof it was done.

Again the demon uttered his threat, and again the disciple wished anew. This went on for some time until finally the exhausted disciple could not think of another thing.

The demon said, "Now I will devour you for sure."

The disciple, with nowhere to turn, called his Guru's name, and he appeared at once.

"Please, please help me master," the disciple pleaded.

Quickly the Guru whispered something. Then the disciple proclaimed to the demon that he had a few more wishes.

"Make a large and straight bamboo pole," he said assuredly, and magically it was done. "Now climb up the pole and when you reach the top climb down the pole and continue to do so until I say stop."

The demon begrudgingly climbed up and down the pole. Many years later he became the most tired demon possible.

He then said to the disciple, "Please have mercy on me I promise never to threaten you again if you command me to stop this endless journey up and down."

"So be it," said the disciple. You may stop now, then depart and never return.

The demon is the mind and the bamboo pole is the spinal column. Lifting and circulating the primal energy through the spine will cause the demon thoughts and emotions to calm down so that the silence of the Self can be perceived.

"Meditation in its pure and simple form is effortless control of the awareness. The beauty of it is that nothing can be forced or demanded. You may have to order yourself to sit and do it, but even that changes. It changes because you have learned that it is a very enjoyable experience, an experience that you want to repeat again and again. Pretty soon you find yourself sitting there for thirty minutes or more. In the beginning you are usually unaware of the depth and power that is available to you; it's just something you like to do. Then you slowly and undeniably start to feel something, a steadily increasing pleasurable inner sensation. It's the bliss current, the balanced current in the center of the spine."

He paused and lit a cigarette, allowing me to ask a question or make a comment.

"I think I am beginning to feel that current," I stated.

"If you have been meditating for the last six months then you should start to feel it," he said.

He knew that I had been doing the Kriyic breath for about six months. It was in fact, the reason that I got to see him. He somehow checked on the people at the temple.

In November of 1968 Swami Kriyananda quietly approached me and gave me Shelly's address. (He didn't have a phone, and as it turned out he never got one in his name). "This is for you and not for the world," he said cautiously. "I understand," I answered, and I kept quiet about it for a while.

It was dark now and the incessant beat of the insects was quite loud. All the doors and windows were open but it remained quite hot. Shelly's house was never air-conditioned, so it always was about 80 to 85 during the day and about 70 by morning.

Lady, the dog, started to growl, ever so quietly.

"Do you think someone is coming over here little girl?" he said without ever looking at her or me.

His eyesight was poor, so he couldn't really see me, at least the physical me. He seemed to be able to direct his inner gaze at me instead. I got very used to this fact and found that eye contact was very over-rated.

"Meditation can be expressed in a formula," he said.

"Formula," I thought," I don't know if I am ready for any formula."

Aware of my sentiment he said, "It's really a basic and simple formula that needs to be understood. Duration times intensity, (D x I), then he quickly added, "And by intensity I don't mean a lot of mental activity. It's the focus and intent of your mind times the length of time you spend in practice," he said.

"Well this seems simple enough," I thought.

"You are the meditator, right?"

He demanded an answer.

"Yes," I said, thinking that it was some trick to make me feel stupider then I already felt.

"O.K., and you have an object of meditation."

"Yes," I said.

"Then there is the act of meditating," he said, with some building affect.

"Yes," I said again."

"I was on a real roll now," was my silly thought.

"So then your goal is what," he added?

"Not to make mistakes," I blurted out."

"No," he said calmly, it's to have a perfect meditation isn't it?"

"Yes," I said, without feeling rejection.

Shelly continued; "So you have the meditator, the act of meditating, the object of meditation. When these three merge, then a perfect meditation ensues. You could also say it's the interplay between the Self and the Not-Self, he added."

I wasn't getting it, but I continued to listen attentively.

"The meditator or M is over the object (O) of meditation and this equals the act or A. When the meditator and the object merge there is no act any more, he said in a matter of fact tone. The person meditating doesn't cease to exist in the perfection of the meditation, does he?" He didn't expect an answer.

"There is a dimensional movement here, and it can be expressed as the square root of minus 1. Through complex numbers you can show how a real entity becomes an imaginary construct and then back again."

He went on for a while on how the meditator, over the act, equals minus O for object, and equally how -O over M = A or act.

I asked Shelly if he could write it down. He agreed.

I sat next to him as he filled a whole page with the equations. (See Appendix A.) Of course he left me very far behind on the first line.

"This equation is something that I developed. If you are discussing meditation with someone who is interested in science it helps explain what is going on," he said.

Marjorie had walked from the kitchen to the bedroom and then back again a number of times. Each time she had a book in her hands. I would turn my head slightly to acknowledge her but there was no exchange of words. This was really good I thought, she is leaving us alone to talk.

Shelly's trend of thought shifted more directly to Kriya Yoga.

"Theoretically Kriya Yoga is the fastest path to Self Realization. It is very scientific in its techniques. They are designed to go directly to the basic flow of currents in the spinal centers. Contrary to what people think, a persons belief system is somewhat immaterial, as long as the spinal currents flow properly. You could be a religious person, an agnostic, or even an atheist," he said.

"Doesn't it matter at all how a person thinks? I asked."

"Not that much. After all, if they are inspired to meditate they have already realized something very important. Meditation will eventually change the way they think anyhow. Look at history, some agnostics were much more humane then the religious bigots," he said.

"There are different types of Yogas. The service path of Karma Yoga is very slow compared to Kriya, he said. Laya Yoga is perhaps the closest in technique to Kriya. The Kriya path is not the best for everyone due to the speed and power of the currents that are released. The dynamic increase in ones Self-conscious awareness can be somewhat unnerving."

"There is also the problem of specific blockages in a person's spinal centers, and these can cause psychic and emotional problems. This is why the teacher much check the Kriyic breath, give mantras and suggest a chiropractor or work on the spine himself. The kundalini can forcefully open the centers in a imbalanced way with the same problems that drugs have caused, he added."

"Most of the true teachers of Kriya don't care about the amount of students they have, they are only interested in the quality of the student. I remember Yogananda saying that when he went to St. Louis to give a lecture and he only found one student, but he considered it a success!"

"Yogananda had a lot of students anyway," I said.

"Yes that is true, he had contacted nearly a million. This was his outer group, in the middle; it was nearer to one hundred thousand. I know his inner group was quite small," he said.

At that moment I realized the obvious; Shelly was part of that inner group.

He stayed on the topic of Kriya Yoga.

"One Kiryic breath is variable, it really depends on the condition of the person, he said. The Kriya is very individualistic; breathing 10 Kriya's can be dangerous for some and breathing 140 not dangerous for others. It all depends on the condition of the person's psychic centers, which is shown in the karmic patterns of their natal chart."

"The intensity of the average students Kriyic breath during Yogananda's time was not that great. Now the average person's Kriya is more intense."

"Most people make noticeable audible sound when they breathe major Kriya."

"Mine is rather quiet," he added.

He paused a moment and stroked the dog a few times. From across the room I could see that the dog's eyes were seemingly now rolling back. It was reacting to a full evening of petting.

"You could omit any or all of the philosophy associated with the actual technique if you wanted too. The important thing is that the results of the technique are scientific fact. The many ideas that are associated with the Kriya are usually O.K. but using the technique; that's where things begin to happen in a big way, he said."

"Some people get impatient with the process. I know at one point Yogananda did."

"He did?" I probed?

"Yes, he got real impatient and he vowed that he was going to get to God consciousness right then and there. He then began to breath Kriya non-stop for many hours. At one point he felt something bumping the top of his head. When he finally opened his eyes to see what it was, he realized it was the ceiling. He pushed on the ceiling and his body went down to the floor, then he would rise back up there again. You see he had breathed so much Kriya that his body was defying gravity. When the lunar and solar spinal currents merge this can happen. Breathe a lot of Kriya and then get on an accurate scale before and after, and you will weigh less".

"You have to remember that Yogananda had been meditating since he was a little boy, plus he had been practicing Kriya for a number of years. This is why he didn't hurt himself, he added."

"He is lucky he was inside", he said, with a face that suddenly turned red.

Shelly begin to laugh quietly, it was a most joy filled laughter.

It became clear that because he was talking about Yogananda he relived the experience at a deeper level.

I had been keeping quiet up till now, fearing that if I asked a question he would decide to challenge me in some fashion, and in doing so this would reveal some personal shortcoming of mine.

Shelly began again with a slight shift in the theme he had been on. "This Guru and Disciple stuff is really overdone. You either are connected to the person or not. Over a period of time it becomes obvious that the special relationship is there", he said.

"Did you know right away that Yogananda was your Guru?" I asked.

"Not exactly, because he was the one who immediately recognized me first. He said: "You have come, you have finally come, I saw you in my dreams and now you are here."

"What happened then?" I inquired.

"Well he just put his arms around me and gave me a big hug. So that was it, we had met."

I could see that his eyes were filled with an undeniable blissful reverence.

"Shelly, do you know when a person comes to see you if they are your disciple or student?" I asked.

There was a very short pause, which seemed longer then it actually was.

"No, not usually," was his answer.

"I ask Yogananda about it in my dreams and then he nods his head yes or no," he explained in a matter of fact voice.

This piece of information made me very happy. It had been 26 years since he had physically seen Yogananda, and 17 years after his departure from this world. Yet, all that time didn't seem to make a difference; their friendship and deep spiritual bond appeared to be as strong as ever.

"You are only a disciple until you reach Self Realization," he said. "Until that time you have a karmic bond with teacher or Guru. When they advance in spiritual knowing, you also advance. Do you see?"

"Yes," I said peevishly.

"Even if the technique were lost, and Kriya died out the future psychic scientists would rediscover it again. It is a basic truth, and so in the balance of Self Realization it will be revealed again." (I wasn't really aware then that he was actually stating a fact of past history. It had been Babaji and only a selected few of his devoted adherents that kept the practice going for a number of centuries).

"Look at the confusing amount of doctrines and theories that are out there now. All you have to do is watch, and wait, and you'll see what is true or not. If they are just cults, well, they usually find a way to hang themselves".

It was close to 10:30 in the evening and Marjorie marched in. With a very certain voice she said, "It's almost time for the Johnny Carson show." She promptly went over and turned on the T.V. She kind of acted like she was interrupting to some degree what was going on. I didn't see it that way and I did welcome her concern.

Johnny's opening jokes were funny and Shelly laughed the hardest I'd seen him laugh. In this laughter his open mouth revealed that there were only a few teeth left. The rest of the show was quite boring. I just sat there and appeared to be interested. I could see that Shelly was doing some of the same. I understood it to be one of their daily rituals they enjoyed doing. I really didn't want to be any kind of disturbance, but I knew that I already had been. After all, nine days is a long time in someone else's house. They had made no mention of a fee or my portion of the groceries, and it didn't seem like they were going too. (I did give them as much as I could afford).

I knew somewhere inside me that I had embarked upon a most remarkable journey. It was an undertaking that would take emotional maturity, mental discipline and an innate fortitude of spirit. What I had to do in order to keep growing was to listen to the loving and wise advise of someone who sincerely wanted to help me. It sounded simple enough but as I have discovered it was one of the most difficult things to do. Our wayward, obstinate, and narcissistic egos really loathed another person's direct advise. The old saying is "the truth hurts," yet it has always been the way humankind has really helped one another.

"If a man does not keep pace with his companions, perhaps it is because he hears a different drummer. Let him step to the music he hears, however measured, or far away"
—Henry David Thoreau

CHAPTER 3.

THOUGHTS ARE THINGS

This was one of those torrential Florida rains that went on throughout the night. I didn't know it then but this area of Florida has the highest amount of lightening strikes in the United States. You could have read a book without the lights being on, that's how bright it got. It was a great natural show. I was a child again with eyes wide open and anticipating the next round of light and sound.

The next morning before breakfast Marjorie gave me the morning news. She said that their water table was high and because of all the rain there was nowhere for the water in the toilet to go.

"So, she said, there's a bucket in there, if you use it let me know."

Why does she want to know if I have used it I thought, and what do I do with it when I do use it? I was already feeling like an immature child and now this was like my potty chair.

Later on I felt a little silly saying; "Majorie, I just used the bucket."

"O.K.," she said promptly entering the bathroom. She took the bucket and rather quickly walked into their wild and natural backyard. I could see that that she had a shovel and was burying the contents. It was just a simple chore for her, something to be dispensed with at once without any thoughts and emotions connected.

It was a lesson in humility, more for me then for her. We became friends after that morning. This was not only required it was a real necessity. After all, she had been with Shelly for over 20 years as his wife. I was incapable of knowing it at that time but she was a fully liberated spirit.

Shelly was more then willing to discuss things at breakfast but he usually didn't elaborate. It didn't matter that much because there never seemed to be an ending to any of his teachings. You got the definite feeling that it was an on-going endeavor. A rare work of art that was somehow just about to be completed. He really had a way of creating suspense and keeping the mystery alive. He didn't do this because of his flair for the dramatic. It was a natural outcome of a life filled with uncommon discoveries and paranormal perceptions.

It was a quiet breakfast until we were just getting up from the table. We heard a car horn, and Marjorie immediately looked out the window.

"Rosner is here," she said in a voice that was both perplexed and amused. As we all went out the back door we could hear his truck sputtering as it slowly came up the driveway. I could easily see a large branch of an oak tree in the back of the pick-up truck. Rosner appeared to be very excited and his usually red face was even redder then normal. He got out of the truck quickly and approached all of us. After a quick introduction and a handshake he addressed Shelly.

"Shelly, I found this branch near to where I live. The tree had been hit by lightening, look here where the branch broke from the tree."

We all approached cautiously. I could see that there was a large amount of sap oozing from the spot where the lightening hit the branch.

"Remember Shelly, you told me that this sap has special magical qualities from the lightening! I could hardly drive over here; it kept interfering with my truck's engine. What should we do with it Shelly."

"I think you should get it out of here," Shelly said seriously while he showed a very broad smile. His mood was somewhere between amusement and irritation.

Rosner's boyish face looked a little disappointed. "O.K. Shelly I'll get rid of it," he said. We all exchanged a few words and off he went in his sputtering truck.

"Rosner is naive about a lot of things," Shelly said.

"Why did he think you wanted to see the sap?" Marjorie added.

"I don't really know," Shelly said. "He gets very excited about psychic phenomena, so it's predictable that he would do something like this," Shelly said.

"He is always buying these strange contraptions."

"What type of contraptions, "I asked.

"You know the ones that they sell in all of the questionable metaphysical magazines," he answered. "He has bought many of them, he brings them over and I test them out," he added.

"Did any of them work?" I asked.

"No, absolutely none, "was his answer. "They all made great claims about their ability to heal or produce some result, but I could not get any to actually work".

"Do you see how gullible and desperate people are?" he said.

"You wonder why they didn't think about it first," I said.

Shelly's face went a little blank and his eyebrows lifted. "Think about it, most people can't think a all," he said with certainty.

"Shelly what do you mean they can't think," I said.

"Just what I said, they are incapable of thinking clearly, and this goes for over 98% of people on earth."

The rebellious youthful part of me loved his statement, but I did feel that he was making a rather extreme indictment of humanity.

"They all think that they are thinking clearly but really they are just emoting", he said. Look, with most people they are emotionally programmed by 5 or 6 year of age. Psychologists have known all this for years," he stated quite convincingly.

I just sat quietly and listened, I didn't want to interrupt his train of thought.

"The average emotional level of most people is about 7 years of age and mentally they are not too far beyond that", he said.

Hoping to keep him on this trend I spoke up.

"So the world is filled with big problems because of this fact."

"Yes, yes, plus the fact that the average person desires only amusements and diversions from everyday life. They don't want to deal with their shortcomings. They like to solve other people's problems with what they call thinking, but with their own problems it's with total emotion," he said.

He anticipated my thoughts, "No one is steering their ship", he said.

He lit a cigarette and changed his topic. "I told you that reality is not what you think it is," he said.

"Yes Shelly I remember that," I said.

"This room, here at this very moment, is filled with television, radio and short wave broadcasts, isn't it?" He didn't wait for me to say yes, he heard me say it mentally.

"Are they interfering with each other?" he asked.

Luckily, I said, "No."

"That is right", he said. There are all kinds of non-physical beings in this universe, so where are they all?" he said.

I was completely unready to answer that one.

"The various waves don't interfere with each other because they all operate at different frequencies. The beings don't interfere with each other because they are in different dimensions. I began to tell you that meditation causes a dimensional movement. You are in a certain dimension right now. In other words, you are in a certain position in time and space. Some other beings can be in that same time and space, but they are dimensionally removed so there is no interference."

"So now you have a beginning idea or concept about the reality you live in, I like to call it one's dream of reality. Most people don't like to get their dream of reality disturbed and this includes you."

"So part of growing spiritually is to get your dream of reality disturbed," I remarked.

"Definitely, if they are wondering in a stupor of unknowing they certainly need to be awakened. But you just can't disturb anyone else's dream. They must ask first. When people seek you out, and attend your classes this is, in fact, a way of asking, so go ahead and disturb them."

"Shelly, it doesn't seem to take much to do it," I said.

"No, it really doesn't take much at all. There are a number of people that want to awaken from their false dream of reality, but like most people they dislike getting disturbed. However on occasion they do manage to disturb themselves."

Without a pause he continued confronting me on my thinking processes.

"Look at the way your mind works now. You have all kinds of imaginative thoughts that you think are logical. Most of them have no objective logic to them but because you give energy to these internalized notions, you right away think they must be

31

understandable and clearly logical to everyone. They are not, he said intensely."

His perception was operating on me in a profound manner and I reacted like a patient who was having a tooth pulled, while at the same time feeling the elation of the pain killer medication. It started with a big smile, which quickly turned into a muffled laughter. I could have easily cried but the joy of the whole situation was more prevalent.

At this very moment Marjorie walked over and chimed in with "Look at how he is laughing."

She said it with no judgment whatsoever. It was more like a comment of an interested bystander, or in this case, the attending nurse. I never had to clarify to Shelly that my strange laughter meant no disrespect. He just understood and continued on with his train of thought.

"You have to learn to express yourself clearly," he added.

"If I keep on meditating, my thinking will continue to change, won't it?"

"Yes, yes it is changing but you must be completely relaxed in the Kriyic technique so that you can go deeper into meditation".

"Well, Shelly, will you check my Kriya?" I asked.

He looked at me indirectly and just quietly said, "Yes," while at the same time he bent his neck to his left. I could hardly hear him say the word yes, so I asked again. This time he just bent his head again. I don't know why but I took this to mean a definite yes.

"Now you see why most male mystics like the solitude of caves. Most of them have a hermit instinct as part of their basic makeup. I like caves myself, but the vast open stillness of the ocean is also quite good too. In the old days if you wanted to find a holy man, you went looking around where there were many caves."

"In the true meditative state a person is thankfully away from this world. You will begin to feel the stillness and solitude from that place and your mind will reprogram itself to think clearly," he announced. Man, in his thinking process, assumes that there is a standard perception of reality. If an event doesn't fit into this pattern, he just quickly forgets it because it doesn't fit into his rigid concept of reality. So when there is something as strange as spontaneous combustion of someone, or the disappearances of individuals, even whole families, well, it's simply pushed to the side and forgotten."

He continued on in the same general area.

"What most people don't realize is that there are many strange erratic time and space warps that are occurring in this world from the world of Ida. In the next few decades the line is going to become thinner and thinner between that world and this one," he stated. (The word Ida was the Kabalistic term he often used for the dream/astral World).

He was moving right along and I had to make a choice whether to ask questions or listen.

After a few seconds he spoke again.

"The distance in time between cause and effect will become shorter and shorter as we move toward the Aquarian Age. Right now in the many parts of the modern world people for the first time, have enough spare time to either meditate or do something wrong." He hesitated an instant to let his statement sink in. "As time goes on, a person's karma will slowly become more fated, and their dream of reality may turn out to be a nightmare. It gets so bad, they forget everything in the green hell"

"The green hell?" I queried.

"Yes, the grave," he said. "The evil that has been done is going to catch up to them, he added. Nature is going to go on a rampage. Remember, it is said, "They will beg the mountains fall on them."

The mood had gotten very apocalyptic and I really wasn't sure who the "they" were. It later became obvious that it was the majority of mankind that he was talking about. At this point in my studies I just couldn't grasp the magnitude of his statements. Also I was completely in the dark about his position in the world and the amount of enemies he had. I was convinced of one thing, I needed to continue to meditate, and it was my only hope.

Wishing to maybe change the subject, I said that meditation was becoming a habit for me.

"That's good," he said.

"You know some of the people I met in California had been coming to hear Yogananda lecture for up to 10 years, and they still were not using the first Kriyic breath!"

"Yogananda taught in his own style. I know that he wasn't very interested in magic for example. He always used to say get the bliss of God-Consciousness first, and then you could investigate other mysteries. So, in his case he wisely by-passed the astral plane in his search. He did like astrology, but not a whole lot."

I intensified my attention hoping that he would continue to talk about Yogananda.

"Before I went to California I knew there were two people out there that taught a special breathing technique, he said."

"Shelly, who was the other one?" I questioned.

"He was an Egyptian mystic in North Hollywood, and he had a number of temples back then. His philosophy was very different from Yogananda's. Well he was out of town when I went to see him so I went over to Yogananda's temple.

He didn't say it, but I could not believe that his meeting Yogananda was just a chance occurrence.

"There were a lot of so called spiritual things going on before the war, some good and others not so good."

"I never heard about the not so good stuff," I curiously asked.

"Black magic," he said directly. There was all kinds of black magic going on in Los Angeles in the twenties and nineteen thirties. There were a number of groups practicing sacrifices, drinking blood and having ritualistic orgies. Charlie Chaplin was the leader of one of the groups!"

"He was supposed to be a funny man," I said.

"Yeah, he was funny alright," he said.

"So Yogananda and others were trying to do good to offset the evil energy in Hollywood?" I said.

"Yes, and do you think they were successful?"

"Well, not really, maybe only in part," I said.

"That is right they were only partly successful," he summarized.

Wanting him to hold his thoughts I asked.

"Shelly, it seems that times were a little different back then."

"I don't know what you mean by different," he said quickly. "I can tell you that I was asked a number of times if I wanted to attend those black rituals and I declined. I did try to make contact with the white brotherhood, but no one would say who or where they were.

There were all kinds of spiritual groups but I couldn't get any of them to admit to being in the white brotherhood."

In a relaxed manner he started to entertain fond memories of that period in his life.

"I really liked the main library there in Los Angeles. They had just about every book I asked for."

"I was doing a great deal of reading back then. I could not afford to buy all those books. I would get so engrossed in reading that I learned how to do it and walk at the same time. The local traffic cop saw me almost everyday and he knew my peculiarities. He on many an occasions, would stop traffic for me. I was usually unaware of this until I was on the other side of the street. Then he would smile and we would say. "Hello."

"There was one house I used to pass that was filled with midgets"

"With midgets?" I said.

"Yeah, they were all midgets, men and woman. I talked to them and they wanted me to join their group. They even said they would pick a wife out for me. Well, I am short but not to the point that I thought of myself as a midget". (He was actually about 5'2" or 5'3" in height) They were all in this house together because they were in a movie together".

I could feel a large smile spreading across my face.

"It wasn't the "Wizard of OZ" was it?"

"Yes, that was the movie, he acknowledged."

This I found to be very funny and Shelly knew it. He didn't seem to care, after all. He laughed to the point of convulsions about the folly of people. I just laughed on the inside and tried to stay attentive.

That night when I was meditating I was about halfway through when I felt like someone was near my left side. It was only a few inches from me. I kept doing my Kriyic breath while I remained conscious of this presence. As I continued to meditate, suddenly I realized that the familiar feeling that came from this presence next to me was the same as Shelly's. It was Shelly in his light body! There was no panic; I didn't even open my eyes. He was checking my Kriya. This was a way that allowed him to attune to the flow of currents in a much clearer way then in the physical.

One day just seemed to happily blend into the next. I was no doubt more in a dream state then any place else. The highlight of the day was the evening when Shelly and I would sit in the living room and talk. Ninety percent of the time I listened, but occasionally I would try and say something coherent. I don't think most of my comments were anything more then emotional matter-of-fact statements. Of course, Shelly would let me speak whenever I wanted to, while he listened on a number levels. He was always amused at my odd and fragmented thought patterns.

"Life is a progression, not a station."
—Ralph Waldo Emerson

CHAPTER 4.

A GOOD LITTLE BIT ABOUT MANY THINGS

It was early evening and the humidity level was very high and the temperature was quite warm too. Both must have been about 80 degrees. Realizing that the heat was really going to affect my tentative concentration level, I asked a question.

"Shelly don't you think it's a little hot?"

"No, not really, I don't feel hot at all," was his answer.

"This is really not hot anyway. But sometimes in August about this time it gets a little uncomfortable," he said emphatically.

I really couldn't believe he wasn't hot. I was in shorts, T-shirt and clogs and the sweat was dripping from me everywhere.

"So what do you consider hot Shelly?" I asked.

"I like it real warm, even California wasn't warm enough. Maybe the surface of Venus would do," he said.

There was no point in adding or further questioning him because his previous statement was so clear.

Spontaneously he began to speak.

"You know, woman are like chlorine atoms and men are like a hydrogen atoms. When they interact the extra electrons from the male/hydrogen atom is transferred to the female/chlorine atom."

"That's a very unusual way of looking at it", I thought.

After this statement Marjorie was in the room in a flash. Shelly was quietly laughing with anticipation.

"You know Shelly has some rather abstract ways of expressing things. Even on our honeymoon night he went into great detail about how lovemaking could be explained very clearly with mathematical equations."

Shelly just kept a big smile on his face. You could tell that Marjorie would from time to time use this same story to illustrate her point. The tone of her voice was neither nagging nor critical. The only conclusion I was left with is that she was gently teasing him about how his mind works.

Shelly started in again, "You know that woman are usually the ones with the maternal instincts. They really don't need men that much, from an Amazonian point of view. What if they froze enough sperm or found a way to be a self fertilizing species?"

"I don't know Shelly," was my brief answer."

"Men have repressed woman for a long time and now the pendulum is swinging the other way," he continued. They are going to have a big role in the coming Aquarian age. If the women become the leaders, then the culture will be very stable. Everyone will be on an equal footing."

"Look how things have changed since I was a boy. My grandmother only went to third grade. "Why educate her any further?," was their attitude. She had been working in the mill from four years of age and was taught how to cook. The men said why waste an education on her. You see how they thought back then?"

"When this new age dawns upon us it could be kind of boring for some men. Remember that your average man is fairly aggressive. Men need to feel they are fighting for something. Like in the old days they went to war for different and more important reasons."

He paused very briefly for a question that I was not quick enough to deliver.

"They went to war to get more woman. Of course it wasn't the only reason. But look at the astrological female symbolism of the Moon and Venus, property, beauty, society, and luxury. Woman are always a symbol of wealth, material and spiritual."

I was just beginning to see his profound appreciation of woman. I also realized that his statements could be easily misinterpreted. In his daily life it was very obvious that he treated Marjorie as a complete equal in a necessary co-equal relationship.

"Male rats will fight to the death for the females and it's the same throughout nature. Even the scent of the females is enough to set them off. So man is an aggressive animal, but as a warrior he falls short."

I could not believe that on the one hand, he was saying that men in general were war-like and now he says they are not. He further clarified his statements.

"There was this young man who came to visit me, he was very typical of the type that I am seeing. I asked him if there were a big war, would he fight? He said, no he would not. Then I said, if they invaded the East coast would he fight then? He said no, he still would not fight. Then I said, if they were within one state from where he lived would you fight? He said, maybe he would fight then. This particular person wanted to join the army!"

"Now an army of woman would be unstoppable. They are the best shock troops because they are agile, intuitive and when properly motivated almost impervious to pain over a long duration. Alexander the Great conquered most of the known world and he had a large contingent of woman who traveled with his army. Look at the Israelis. They draft woman and their army is ranked quite high."

I felt the need for him to clarify something, so I asked, "Shelly, by aggressive do you also mean sexual?"

"Yes, that is one expression of the problem, plus most men think they are great lovers. They are not, just talk to their partners. However there are a few men that are highly sexed."

I could feel that a story was brewing.

"This is the gospel truth. I met this man down here when he was sixty-eight years old. He told me that with his first wife, he liked to make love three times a day. It was too much for her and she divorced him. The judge granted the divorce when he heard the number of times he wanted to have sex everyday. Then he found a woman who was agreeable to his particular temperament. He made love to her three times a day till he was seventy-three and had a heart attack. He told me that he was not the man he used to be because now he could only make love to his wife twice a day."

Tongue in cheek, I said, "that was really terrible."

"His wife told me that he made love to her twice a day till he was eighty-two. Then he had another heart attack and was hospitalized for six weeks. After that he told me that he thought he was going to die. I asked him how he knew that. He said, "that it's," because he could only make love to his wife once a day, so he knew it's time to leave! Shortly after that he did, in fact, die."

"There are all kinds beings of out there but if you are lucky enough to meet your twin soul, then you really have something. It is one essence eternally functioning as if they are two, male and female."

"In marriage the Self that you are viewing is symbolically or actually the same Self. Therefore, to the man, a woman becomes the negative factor and accordingly the power holder. Now, she can add and subtract both positive and negative in equations. Like, if you say go, she says stop. If you say up, she says down, and this is what most men call being contrary. This, by itself, does not cause many problems. But when she wants to control and use the power, usually against the man, then a whole new equation is in place. Depending on the situations, it can be tolerable unless it goes into multiplication. When this happens the emotions rule and not the intellect and all kinds of problems arise."

The abstractness of his statements were both puzzling and interesting but I lacked the skills for carrying the discussion further.

"The old saying is that a man chases a woman until she catches him."

"If you are successful in life, it will be so because of a good female companion. Behind every great man is a great woman, driving him onward. A person is not a single person anymore when married. Your auras blend, so your actions are not entirely dependent on you alone, but on your mate as well. A woman usually does most of the sacrificing, while men are kind of insufferable creatures filled with inconsiderate actions.

"So Steve, if you marry the right woman, you will grow spiritually and if you marry the wrong woman, you will grow tremendously."

We both let out a quick chuckle. Then he related another story.

"There once were two young men who were both in love with the same woman. They both did everything they could think of to win her affections. Finally the time came that she had to make a decision of which one she would marry. The guy who lost out took it very hard. He knew in the entire world, that his greatest enemy was the man she had chosen. A number of years later he was visiting his hometown. While walking down the street he saw the same man approaching with a woman. He then recognized that the woman was his lost love, but she had put on at least 150 pounds. He watched while she continued to yell at her husband and take swipes at him with an umbrella. He knew then, that in the entire world, his greatest friend, was this man."

All I could manage was a slow, "Wow."

Wanting to tease his wife, he injected a radical view.

"It all depends on how many wives's you want. The Mohammedans say one wife is not enough. If you have two they just fight with each other. Having three wives means that two will gang up on the one. Four, they say is best because they take sides and pair up into a favorable truce. This makes the house peaceful and keeps you out of any conflict," he said smiling.

"Now, on the Yoga path there needs to be certain periods of celibacy in a person's life. Lahiri Mahasha recommended that a man should start to become more and more celibate during his forties."

Mildly laughing he said, "Look at Gandi; he finally proved that he was celibate when he was so old that he was becoming impotent."

"Of course, there is another type of teacher that is only too willing to help woman out sexually."

"Yes Shelly, they call them the "divine orgasmic type." It's one aspect of Tantra Yoga to surrender, rather then kill desire"

"Yea, I know. Some of them say no sex except with me! There's a group in Tibet that takes herbal stimulants. They have sex until they are completely exhausted then they claim they can enter a very deep trance. Tell that to a young man, and that's where he will want to go. You see there are all kinds of paths to Self-Realization."

"The danger is that physical sex is still a function of the lower three centers, and especially the solar plexus which can be purely a sexual function. It has a way of enslaving people. But most people still get married on that basis alone. It's a compulsion, and it doesn't seem to matter where they are in the world when the time is right it happens. It seems to be an acceptable hormonal insanity that can last up to three years. I have seen this over and over again in people's charts."

"In order for they're to be love, the cardiac center must be activated. If you have that center firing, and higher ones, then it can be real love. By that I mean varying degrees of unselfish love, like with soul mates and twin souls. So I tell people to enjoy life, but be cautious."

41

"Many cultures have tried to repress people's sexual appetites. It has never really worked. After all we do have these human bodies, which operate on glandular secretions."

"Again, what is really important is the control and flow of the currents between partners. If they can make their individual loops of energy one, then the retention of the seminal fluid is not that important."

"I have told you I have seen them making love in the high astral plane. One ball of light is blue and the other is green. They merge and you can feel their bliss. Afterward, they are both purple for awhile."

"Then there are children. They pick up most of the emotional programs from their parents. I have been a parent in one way or another to twelve of them. One of the most important parts of raising children is discipline. They have to be disciplined in a fair and consistent manner, and it must start early. If they are not, it will cause instabilities in their nervous system. Naturally later on this leads to behavioral problems. They will not respect their parents, and they will manipulate the situation whenever possible."

"Sometimes physical discipline is necessary, especially with boys. But you should not spank them when you are really angry."

I immediately said to myself, 'Well, when would be a good time?" Later I realized the wisdom of making a good attempt at being neutral and impartial.

"Back in the nineteen-twenties, in an experiment, they raised a number of children with no discipline at all. They felt that discipline was a form of repression and it would damage their delicate personality complex. As it turns out, there was only one child in the whole group that turned out to be very successful, and that was Orson Wells. However, no woman, or actually anyone, could stand to live with him."

"All good parents want to protect their children. You can't deny that the supernatural is real, let them know that. When you meditate you can cover them with love and light. But they must learn to protect themselves. The mother becomes very important. It cannot have survived without her. This deep ancestral worship works. When the child calls out for mother, or thinks about her, the child automatically sets up a protective field around itself. It varies, depending on the circumstances and awareness level of the child"

*　　　　*　　　　*

I had been noticing for some time now the strange little light flashes and bubbles that were present in the room. I was not able to focus on any of them. I noticed them only intermittently, but just enough to remember them. They appeared for only a brief second, and often in my peripheral vision. On this trip Majorie had told me that every so often the neighbors would call public service to report various types of lights that appeared above and next to the house. Of course they always investigated, but found everything to be normal.

Shelly opened up another new trend of thought.

"We, on this earth, are missing a great deal of information. There is a tremendous amount of hidden knowledge we don't know about. Many times the limited knowledge we do have gets confused in translations. This is why the real knowledge is in symbols. There are a number of unique symbols, and sacred languages, which are actually based on math."

The occult, more then any other field, is filled with useless information. You can't prove or disprove many of the theories. In other words there are many so-called truthful statements that have no real practical value. I once heard a person say; Love is something divine willed by the hand of God. It's a nice statement but it says nothing."

I did feel it said something, but I had to agree with him. In reality, it said very little. I made no comment.

He continued with an unusual certainty.

"Most occult or spiritual organizations are pure plagiarism, often using ghostwriters. It's a very disturbing aspect for people who are truly seeking. You see, almost all so-called prophets are self-proclaimed. Given enough time they are either proved or disproved. Yogananda once said that he would give anyone ten thousand dollars if they could disprove he was a Yogi."

43

"In the olden days, many centuries ago, most of mankind was real psychic. They had many spirtual talents, but some used them for there own benefits. Instead of using them to grow spiritually, they used them to gain greater power and money. To go down that road can get you weeded out of God's cosmic dream. Be assured, that eventually everyone gets confronted one way or another."

"Look at dying, for example. Usually the shock and release at death causes a necessary debriefing. A radiant being asks you; "What did you learn and was it worth it?" So, you see, for many it's painful to live in a body and equally painful to give it up.""

"My advice to you is to go out into the desert where nobody lives and drill a 1000 foot well. Sometimes the best way to help people is be away from them. You know Nostrodamus had his doorknobs charged with a homemade static electricity contraption so that he would not be awakened or disturbed while in trance.""

I thought that I knew what he meant by "weeded out", but as it turns out I only had a superficial understanding of it. I only smiled a little about his discreet comment, because I wasn't sure what he was suggesting.

Then he summarized with an equally relevant tidbit.

"People are very ego-centric, they feel they are the center of the universe. Of course this is actually true to some extent. What they fail to realize is that it is also true for everyone else too! Space is curved, so this automatically makes this so."

He did not explain himself further about curved space.

Instead he decided to state, "You are aware that you are, but what are you aware of? Whatever it is, you are more aware of it then others or the others would be you. If anyone can convince you, that you are not really you, then you will cease to exist!"

This was definitely one of his little mind bending quotes. As usual, some of the implications were threatening, as well as being profound. Before I could regain my composure, he continued.

"God made man, and then he thought that mankind would naturally seek out their divine nature, because after all they were part of him. Where shall I put this immortal spark he thought? Shall I put it in the earth, or in the quasars? I have it, I'll put it in his very own Self, he may never think of looking for it there!"

Reeling from his remarks, I managed to formulate a question.

"Shelly with all of these problems do you think that mankind will get to the Aquarian Age?

Without hesitation, he answered, "Yes."

"But keep in mind that the Aquarian age is really the dream of Man. It is not necessarily, wholly, the dream of God. The concept of God as father will change to God as brother and sister. There will still be problems in that age. Man could begin to think that he alone is God. Yet there will be a great many people who will seek the truth. Many of these will become Self-Realized or God Conscious."

"Along with all of this, the future sciences will be almost unimaginable in their scope. Beings will travel from the earth to Arcturus and come back the day before they left!"

Then, in his usual unannounced fashion, he gave me a helpful warning.

"If you plan to reincarnate again in that time, make sure you have an extremely difficult horoscope".

"Why would I want a difficult chart?" I inquired.

"Because life will become unbelievably easy. Everything will be taken care of; all of your needs will be met. On the whole, people will be quite spiritually evolved compared to the present. They will have a very different view of time, and so they may become indifferent to their minor imperfections."

"A hard chart is very energizing and motivational. It will instill within a person the need to continue to grow in spite of any and all conditions."

"The present way our time sequences work, allows for many distortions. Super civilizations have balanced time sequences. Therefore we have a communication problem."

Lets say you make a decision at a certain point in time. You feel that it is a really good decision. Then 10 years later you can see that it was the worst decision you could have made. Then after a 100 years it doesn't matter what decision was made."

Then he quickly added, "It is difficult to look into the future and point out exact reference points relative to the time scale we have now. I have likened it to having 1000-watt and 60-watt light bulbs that are out in front of you at a distance. Both represent a future event.

45

Now you tell me which one is actually the closest? Sure the 1000 watt bulb may "appear" to be closer but is it really closer?"

"In one sense the future is already written. Time and space are moving toward each other. The Aquarian Age was written before it began. If you have enough self-conscious awareness then you can alter the future. But you have to know about the possibilities first. In the average person, what we call the present overlaps the past and the future. When someone is more spiritually developed the overlap is greater. So there is less uncertainty because they can see farther. They see more of the representative symbols. When the symbol sequence is changed you can alter future events. But to what degree can this be done, that is the big question?

"There are also certain ancient discrepancies about time. We could be living 4 years farther in the future then where we think we are!

"Now a large number of seers have seen very difficult times ahead at the closing of this present age. Many, many of the possibilities have been written about. What exactly will happen is open. But one thing we can be sure of, is that when so many over a long period of time have seen trouble, then we know that something of a difficult nature will likely transpire."

Then he related a frightening probability.

"Do you know what an electro-magnetic pulse is?"

"I kind of know," was my answer.

"Everyday, more and more information is being stored on computers. Well this pulse will wipe out all the stored information if you are in its range. Any atomic bombs or even asteroid hits will do this."

"A number of worldwide plagues and famine are other possibilities. Before WWII the Aurora Borealis was covering all of Europe. Now I have seen its fingers extending down over the United States, especially the Mississippi Valley."

"Observe what happens to the population curves with any organism. There are just too many people on the planet, something has to give."

"Look at how nations act as little children and how religions cause people to go to war. All this shows you the low maturity level of humanity in general."

"People are always asking me where the safest place is to be. I answer by telling them it's in a craft off the planet's surface."

"Yogananda was always telling people to live naturally and simply. He would say, grow your own food, live in the country and have a food storage area. He was saying this back in the late 1930s. All of his centers had big gardens, and the students would have contests on who could grow the most in their plot."

"All these prognosticators feel they are right and that they have a great track record. So which one do you pick?"

"There is a lot of controversy about just when the Aquarian age will begin. The astronomical and astrological measurements vary by several hundred years. But if you look at it from a purely symbolic and astrological viewpoint, then the Aquarian age can't be too far in the future."

"Great souls now mostly incarnate in North America, Europe and China, a few in Brazil. In the future they will be in many places on and off this planet. Yogananda told me that in the distant future man would live fifty to one hundred thousand years in one lifetime and in the same body. It was that way in the distant past. The Sumerian records are dated 50,000 years before the flood."

"So man has been here quite a long time?" I asked.

"Yes, much longer then most are willing to admit. The first major civilization was Hyperborean, it was in the Polar Regions."

"Was it the Garden of Eden?"

"It could have been. You know Eve was not Adam's first wife, it was Lilith," he quickly added."

"Who was she?" I asked.

"In the symbolic story she was one of Lucifer's wives, her name was Lilith. He saw how pleased God was with his creation of Adam Kadom, so he lent her to Adam. Then God made Eve and this was an insult to the Archangel Lucifer. He instructed Lilith to fly away. They say she had wings and webbed feet. Adam and Lilith had already had children. Then Adam proceeded to have children with Eve. She had two sons, Cain and Able. As you know Cain killed Able, he then took a wife and went to the land of Nod. The woman he picked was his half sister, a daughter of Adam and Lilith."

"The Free Masons call themselves the "widowers" because they believe they are the descendents of Adam and Lilith. That being the offspring of the original Adam Kadom and the, then, unfallen angels. Lucifer cursed all the offspring of Adam and Eve. So you have three races or basic genetic strains". The offspring of Adam and Eve, Adam and Lilith and...

"What's the third one?" I interrupted.

"That's when the sons of Gods saw the daughters of Earth and found them exceedingly fair," he answered. The fallen angels and all those phony Gods and Goddesses, like in Greece and other places".

His chest heaved a bit.

"So, we are all mixed up genetically from the original intent of the Cosmic Dreamer. In short, the human race has been tampered with."

I knew that it was only part of a larger story, but the best I could do was try to remember the gist of the story. I remained fairly well zapped from the implications of all he had said earlier.

Exuding sternness he directed a question at me.

"So, why do you think you are here?"

"You mean Earth," Shelly?"

"Yes, yes Earth."

"Well, because like everyone else, my karma has kept me in the cycle of reincarnation."

I felt a brief instant of pride with my answer.

"It's not all your direct karma, you lost a war. All involved lost in a great war in the heavens."

Although he did not say it, I intuited the idea that there were a number of wars between various factions.

"One third of the planets and the angelic beings formed a confederacy."

"You see Earth was a spaceship, then moving through dimensional space and time. There was a thick protective ice shield around it. Earth was trying to escape, when a "thought bomb" hit; that's a highly concentrated thought form, with a target. The gravitational energy from earth completely destroyed a close by planet named Lucifer. All that's left is the asteroid belt."

There was a part of my mind that realized this all sounded like science fiction, yet it rang true inside me.

Shelly immediately responded with an assertive reassuring, "I am not kidding you."

"The bomb (missile) had a disastrous effect on the memory track of people. At one moment they were sitting behind the controls that moved the earth and the next moment they forgot what they were doing and why they were there. The ice shield melted and flooded the whole planet. That was really something, because that ice was created under pressure and it would not melt even at 200 degrees F. The rainbow was given as a promise, because before that time there was no interaction between Sunlight and rain. The surface temperatures were uniform back then, and condensation watered the earth. Electromagnetic waves acted like Sunlight. In Egypt they wrote about Sunlight that cast no shadow."

His little black dog was now wide-eyed and very alert. It actually seemed that she was enjoying the story, as well.

"So now there is one more glorious and decisive war to come."

"The old headquarters, location back then, was under Tianica in the Peruvian Andes. That's where the controls (were) are located. There are all kinds of rumors of tunnels and caverns within the many miles of Inner Earth. People are slowly rediscovering bits and pieces of information."

"Did you know that two of the Moons of Mars were described in "Gulliver's Travels," this was many years before their actual discovery. Then there's the Perry/Reis map, it showed almost all of the coastlines in the America's and Antarctica. This was centuries before they were explored."

"There was a female scientist who visited me once, and she told me she saw a huge triangle under the ice cap, he added."

I felt like I should say something out of common courtesy but I refrained from doing so. As I found out later on, if you felt you were having a so called normal conversation with Shelly, you were in fact harboring certain illusions. He never tried to dominate a conversation; neither did he show any intellectual smugness. It's just that the exchange of words was not the major part of what was actually going on.

"A number of beings have keep us under observation. They can clearly see that we have a crude technology. We still use the brute force method for many things."

"Many of these UFO's that are seen are real. When you can track their positions on two or three radar screens at the same time, they have to be real. Some of these visitors use anti-gravity craft."

"They have mastered energy and mass, oscillating it to effect time and space. It's a standing wave motion using positive and negative time (L over T). This allows for space travel, which is theoretically faster then light."

"You've read part of the Ray Palmer material; he felt that some of those civilizations had weapons that can wipe out whole planets. Certain Russian scientists believe they can harness the fusion energy of three Suns. They also believe that Jesus was a spaceman from somewhere else.

"I just sat there with strong and mildly pleasurable sensitivities in the back of my head. I also had that tasteless taste under my tongue. It was close to the same phenomena I experienced while under the influence of hallucinogens.

"So we are the rebels, and this is our gravity world, a prison planet," he lamented.

"It's a prison," I thought out loud.

"Yes, all gravity worlds can be that way. Lets examine it: you have to consume close to one half a ton of food in a year's time. Then you have to spend about one third of your life resting your body. By the time the brain matures in the fifties and sixties the body usually gives out. Plus our memory tracks are frozen. This is a very limiting environment!"

It's like some people say, "Life's difficult and then you die."

"Yea, then you die, or at least you think you are dead. Of course you are still alive when you are dead. They are not any smarter over there for the most part either. You see you can't be in heaven unless you create a little heaven here first. This is why they say only the blind can see, only the deaf can hear, and only the dead can know."

"Many religious people, during their life, expect gifts from God. All right, so then you have a gift from God. Isn't it better for you to get to really know the one God who is the giver of all gifts?"

There was really nothing I could say at that point. However he did have one closing comment.

I had mentioned a particularly powerful and haunting statement made by Nostrodomus. He said it would take place in the final time of earth's transformation. "Many rare birds would yell, Now, Now, Now."

"This is like the "Bride of Christ" concept. The transfinite SEO (Self Existing One's) will leave before and during the disasters, and the opening of the seven seals."

"We made to many wrong mistakes."

—Yogi Berra

CHAPTER 5.

AVATAR OF LOVE

I sat there in Shelly's simple living room waiting for him to sit across from me. I anticipated another spellbinding discourse and I would not be disappointed. I wanted it to go on forever. I knew that these emotions were fanciful and basicly unrealistic. The reality of the situation was that I was really suffering form memory overload and a strange psychic indigestion. I was neither really physically sick, nor tired, just overwhelmed with new ideas and tantalizing possibilities.

I began the nights discussion with what I thought was a legitimate question.

"Shelly why don't you have a temple or an organization?"

"I don't have a temple because of what Yogananda told me."

"What was that, I inquired."

"When I was leaving California he looked me straight in the eyes and said: "You stay free." I instantly knew what he meant. He didn't want me to get all tangled up in an organization. We both had realized that it was not something that I definitely had to do. He also was going to write a chapter about me in "Autobiography of a Yogi," but he changed his mind. As far as teaching goes it was understood that I should teach, but keep quiet about it."

"Most teachers and groups have all kinds of problems because they don't know the basic laws of Self Conscious Awareness, he added."

"Any being, anywhere in existence, that has Self Conscious Awareness, will eventually find these laws to be true."

He quickly fired a question at me.

"Do you remember these laws as they apply to meditation?"

I wanted so much to answer him with a clear and crisp voice but all that came out was a series of "I"s and "A"s.

"OK so you have forgotten already?" he said.

"Yes, Shelly, I said meekly."

"It's the meditator over the object and the act of meditation which equals the power of meditation or one perfect meditation."

I gave a resounding "Yes" but it did not recoup my losses.

He continued unperturbed.

"When you meditate on things they consume energy. Thoughts are things aren't they? When you meditate on the Self this gives energy. The Self is nothing or no thing.

The object of beauty, Guru, and the blue light are all still things. The Self is neither the ego, body or thoughts you think."

"When you can maintain 51% of your awareness on the Self you are instantly immortal. What I mean by that is you realize your "conscious immortally". You are in fact immortal right now, but you are not fully conscious of it."

I focused intently on his words.

"Your concept of Steve is a very minor dream in the vast spiral of time. You only have a few percentage points of awareness now."

He didn't verbalize his remaining thoughts but I felt he was saying; "So what are you going to do about it."

He was confronting me, and at that point I could only accept his challenge. There was no other way for me to go at that stage. Excuses were unacceptable and I knew it.

"Basically the Guru is the one who has the abstract concept about consciousness. The disciple doesn't have it yet but when he gets it they are both free from one another. It's not a question of who has more or less, concepts don't exist in the susamonic/ balanced state."

"The basic statement that was used by the ancients was; "I am aware that I am". This is what the true Self is saying. Yet most people are only aware of things within their dream of the not-self."

I continued to remain quiet.

"I have noticed that the majority of people have four basic drives. They desire a certain amount of importance. They want to be loved. They crave a certain amount of change. Lastly they want things to go on forever. Living a type of physical immortality. Of course most people will deny any or all of these. Yet given the proper circumstances these drives become very apparent."

"The biggest problem is that mankind is loaded with selfish love. This type of love is completely different from God's love. God's love is unselfish love. It's unselfish love without any force field associated with it. The bliss is an ever new, ever changing and ever more glorious bliss. All he or it wants to do is to share this with us. It is the most complete state of giving possible."

"Mystics who have felt this unconditional love have been capable of great sacrifice," he added.

I explained to Shelly the story I heard of the three soldiers in Viet Nam. They were all in a foxhole together when a grenade was thrown in. Without any hesitation one of the three jumped onto it, whereupon it immediately exploded.

"This will create a tremendous amount of good karma for that individual. He didn't have time to think, so he had to react with his whole being. It would have been an act of unselfish love whether it exploded or not," he said.

"In their relationships with children, women are often unselfish. Their heart and hormones are strongly inclined toward this expression. Every time a mother acts with the feeling of unselfish love, she is at that moment closest to Cosmic Dreamer or God."

"So you are saying that woman are closer to God then men."

"Yes, when they are in that state they would have to be."

With a distinct certainty in his voice he continued.

"A woman's nervous system is very subtle and highly keyed. They are more naturally intuitive then most men. Woman have an edge over men because of these factors."

"Once a woman shows her hand. That she really has the power, then some men will want to leave. Most men don't want to get married in the first place."

A question immediately welled up in me.

"Shelly, are you saying woman take power or they have power?"

"Magically speaking, the woman holds the power. This has always been so, and it shall no doubt remain that way. The man, depending on his abilities, can use the power.

But he must do it with caution, respect and dignity. If he doesn't, he is in big trouble."

"In nature look how males strut around and show off. They have to be demonstrative because they lack power. The average man is a physical and spiritual weakling compared to a spiritual woman."

"So what is a woman's weakness," I inquired.

"The temporary vessel that holds the power; their bodies. Despite all their advanced stealth they get stuck. They become quite comfortable with the hormonal programming of their bodies."

"Its all part of being human," he continued.

"It is very problematic to be human. We are in quite a predicament for the foreseeable future.

"Not if people become more spiritual," realizing that I stated the obvious.

"That's right but how and when they will decide to awaken is an unknown factor."

Things got quiet for a while. I listened to the fish tank bubbles and the persistent insects sounds. Then he began again and concluded his train of thought.

"Look at Yogananda he was a very commanding man, but he was very aware of his softer side. He was quite capable of being very gentle and loving.

Suddenly his mind shifted to a related topic.

"Kriya Yoga is not evangelistic, it does not believe that you have to go out and find people and convert them. It is an ancient method whereby people are naturally drawn of their own accord. You simply make yourself available by announcing that you are teaching. That's it; they come if they want to."

"In this way every Kriya Yoga teacher becomes a symbol."

Anticipating my question he answered it before I could ask.

"What is the teacher a symbol of? He or she is a symbol for the very thing that the seeker is supposedly searching for. Yet they already have what they are seeking. So basically you really can't teach them anything anyway."

Now my mind was desperately trying to grasp what he was saying.

"They have to ask for this, and this asking can make them aware, on some level, of what they already have, and what they want again."

"You see what I mean Steve?"

"Yes, I think I know what you are saying, Shelly," was my tentative answer.

"You are serving as a mirror, which allows them to see themselves. After all the truth is already within them. So a teacher becomes a mirror of their very own Self-reflection."

"When they are not satisfied with their life they will begin to seek. What they are looking for is a teaching, which is in harmony with a state of awareness they are not fully conscious of yet."

"All who truly seek will then start to gain valuable experiences. They will naturally begin to go through the many stages of Self Realization."

It all seemed so easy for him to say. It was also easy for me to accept. But I did not fully comprehend all of what he was saying.

"I know that I ramble on. It's because everything eventually leads to everything else. I do get back to the original question but who knows how long that will take.

Then for some reason Yogananda came into my mind again.

"Shelly, did Yogananda attempt to explain various mysteries in his teachings?'

"Yes, he did, but most of the time he kept things rather simple in his temple lectures. With his inner group, he would go deeper into hidden matters, if you asked him. Sometimes he would not talk about things because the mere spiritual and intellectual speculation was not high on his list. He had a very devotional personality, so he didn't like to split hairs, so to speak. He felt that the love of God and the ever-new bliss of God consciousness was the most important thing."

"Now with Sri Yutiswar it was different. He was a very advanced scientist. Because of this temperament Yogananda actually felt he was a little cold. I don't know if I told you, but when Yogananda first arrived to live at Sri Yutiswar's Ashram he was given the job of scrubbing the pots and pans. This was quite a blow to someone who was born within the higher part of the caste system."

"Sri Yutiswar also told Yogananda that he had one bad fault. He said, "You have to be told something three times, before you know that you have been told anything"

"You see, in the India of old they liked to teach you personal lessons. If you did too much of that today you would lose all your students."

I could imagine his memory going somewhere.

"Yogananda had two parts to his personality."

"Two parts," I repeated.

"Yes, there was Yogananda the saint and Yogananda the man. The man part was much like his horoscope showed. The saint part was quite different and it was the part that was in control. I have seen him under a number adverse conditions and the saint always stepped in to successfully deal with the situation."

"I'll tell you a story about it," he said.

I was of course all ears for that. As far as I was concerned, all Yogananda stories, had to be great stories.

"Yogananda had ordered a very prized artifact. It was a statue, from Europe or India, I don't remember which. He talked about ordering it, and he mentioned it often enough so that everyone knew it was something he really was looking forward too. Well finally the day came when he received word that it arrived up in San Francisco. He was so excited and happy. He was literally bouncing around full of glee. He picked me and one other disciple to take a truck up there and bring it back."

"We loaded the crate very carefully on the truck and secured it with ropes in a number of ways. We wanted to make sure that we could bring it back safe and sound to Yogananda. We were really looked forward to making our Guru happy."

"No sooner had we begun our journey south then it started to rain. The storm got more intense with a lot of rain and wind. Both of us took turns driving while we kept an eye on the crate. We checked it so many times then at one point we didn't look back for a short period of time."

"When we looked back again it had disappeared. Naturally we really panicked.

We turned around and begin to drive very showly while looking along the roadside for the large crate. Well, we looked for hours, but we never found the crate. We were both quite upset and very depressed over the situation."

"What would we tell Yogananda, how could we possibly explain how a heavy crate just disappeared off the back of the truck? We were absolutely miserable and fearful by the time we got back to the ashram at Encinitas."

"As soon as Yogananda saw our faces, he right away surmised what had happened. We did our best to explain what had occurred but he cut us short. In turn he wrapped his arms around each of us. Then he looked us in the eye and said, "The most important thing is that both of you are safe.""

At this point I could feel tears welling up within me without actually crying. Then instantly I felt a wave of unselfish love sweep across the entirety of my being. It was very real, but not so easy to explain.

Shelly then finished telling the story.

"Yogananda never mentioned the event again. He treated us the same without the slightest hint of what had occurred. So you see Yogananda the saint stepped in and changed the whole situation."

"Now Yogananda the man that was another story. He sometimes acted like he was a Maharaja, you know, like a royal king from India. Yogananda the man loved pomp and ceremony. He loved to entertain dignitaries and serve extravagant meals. He enjoyed all kinds of exotic vegetarian delicacies. He had a lot of fun with his parties."

"He had a very dominant personality but as far as what I saw the Saint was always the part that stood out."

"It sounds like it was a fun time," I added.

"Oh, it was. It was helpful to see it all on a number of levels too. Instead of Master, Master, Master, all the time."

"We really liked each other very much. Yogananda was a very interesting person and like me he had a very strange sense of humor."

"He did," I stated with a smile.

"Yes, he used to wear a raccoon coat, derby hat, and a cane. He wore it all the time when he walked over to do his temple lectures. He did this even in the summer. It was the most fashionable men's wear at one time and he wanted to make a statement."

"He used to repeat often, "we are all actors on the stage of life." As I have told you, time is standing still; you are the actor moving through it. He was very conscious that he was the actor, and he played his role to the hilt."

"He composed a lot of his own music from the Upanishads and other scared texts. He often played the concertina. But he played at a much higher octave then he could sing. He did have a unique voice but if anyone went into God consciousness while listening, it was a great accomplishment."

He gave out an intense short burst of laughter.

"He really liked what he called, "the shoot-em-up cowboy movies". He used to load up two or three cars full of students and go to the movies. He said, "I know they are violent, but at least the moral of the stories are good.""

"Then, at other times when it was hot he would take a large number of female devotees to the all white beach. He would then proceed to instruct them in a series of Hatha Yoga exercises. He was, of course an East Indian Caucasian but his skin pigmentation was very dark."

"I asked him why he did this, and he said he wanted to irritate the other people on the beach by being the only Negro man with all those white woman. "Look… they do everything," he says.

"In many of his talks he conveyed the idea that he really loved America, maybe even as much as India. He knew if they worked together great things could happen for the world."

Without a pause he continued with a large smile and a red face.

"One time there was this young couple, they had just gotten married. They were attending a lecture of Yogananda's; at the temple in L.A. Well his sense of humor got the best of him. At some point in the lecture he went on and on about the virtues of living the life of a celibate. He stressed the importance of conserving sexual energy and that it was misused by so many. You should have seen the faces on the newly-weds. Some would say it was a mean thing to do. I don't think so; there could have been a hidden reason behind his buffoonery."

"That organization kept him real busy, too busy as far I was concerned. He tried to talk with his disciples when he could. If he deemed that you were not receptive, then it was a long time before you spoke with him again."

"He had a unique ability to "read while you run". He could read body language, speech, plus see things psychically. Yet, he had a hard time remembering anyone's name!

"His healing powers were quite pronounced too. I remember there was a woman and a young man that Yogananda had given healings to a week or so before they saw each other again. He asked the woman if she was feeling better. She said yes she was and she gave him two one hundred dollar bills. Then he went over to the man and asked the same thing. He said he wasn't feeling better yet. Then Yogananda put one hand on the man's stomach and one on his spine and meditated for a few minutes. The man then gave him a two-dollar bill. So I asked Yogananda, "Was the lady helped more quickly because she intended to give two hundred dollars? Yogananda said, "it may look that way but she can afford what she gave. The man, he continued, tried to kill himself a few weeks ago, so the healing currents did not flow well within him"

I sat there thrilled by his highly personal reflections.

"Yogananda used to tell us all that there was really only a thin line of difference between him and us. I don't think many of them really understood. Anyway, he never felt he had enough disciples or enough time to teach them.

"But he was happy, wasn't he?" I asked.

"Oh sure, he was always laughing and smiling, yet there was always an undeniable deep inner presence."

"But he did have to work very hard within the organization he created. I know sometimes it was an eighteen-hour day. He tried very hard to run it like a business without making a business out of it. He told me it was a critical balancing act and that he was sure that he had gone over the deep end at times."

"You see he was a great teacher who was capable of sacrificing himself so that others could be saved. However, with most people they are more then willing to sacrifice others for themselves."

"He did require that his disciples give of themselves. The order he gave was information first, then money, followed by service.

"You would be surprised just how many people have wanted to come down here to see me. I have had to keep some away or I would get no rest at all."

Then he added, "They would have killed me long ago."

"The average student is egocentric and very selfish. They think they are the most important being on the face of the earth."

We both sat there while I nervously did a quick examination of my recent actions.

"He was the Guru and he had to always keep an eye out for problems. Many times the students would ask about the astral worlds. He always would advise them not to go there, but to continue concentrating on their meditations. He would say, "Get God Consciousness first." Then you will really see the astral worlds, but not from preconceived ideas." You see most of them were not trained observers. You can easily get caught, because there are all kinds of things to intrigue and entice you there.

"Yogananda did feel the need to get away, this I know for sure. In fact he literally ran away a few times."

"Wow, he did" shot out of my mouth.

"Yeah, he ran away to Mexico three times that I knew about. There was this valley there; he said it was the most beautiful valley he had ever seen. He would try to hide but it wasn't that easy being Yogananda. The longest he was away was two weeks. They always seemed to be able to find him. Sometimes it was the same people that felt compelled to ask what color dress they should wear for a certain occasion. They would leave no stone unturned looking for him. Then when he was back in California they pestered him with a lot of dumb questions."

"Now not all of disciples were like this. There was the one we called "Sister," brother Bernard, Saint Lynn. All of these and some others had already experienced God Consciousness."

"Many times when Yogananda would just touch Mr Lynn he would immediately go into cosmic consciousness! So naturally everyone started calling him Saint Lynn. He was a very successful businessman. He told me by the luck of being in the right place at the right time, he secured a position. But then he had to work incredibility hard just to keep the position. Then over a period of time he became quite wealthy. So he must have done the same with Kriya Yoga. He took advantage of the opportunity, but this time he won true freedom.

"Shelly, when you were there did you have enough time to speak with Yogananda?"

"Just barely. I had to devise a number of plans to be able to speak with him."

At that moment Marjorie stepped in.

"So tell him what you did dear," she requested.

He paused for a few seconds and contemplated her loving demand.

"Whenever he could, Yogananda used to have breakfast with his students. I felt this was a good time to talk with him. It was right after his morning meditation and before he got busy with the rest of the day.

Almost all of the disciples stayed in the dorms. So at night I used to fly through there."

"Fly Shelly?' I asked.

"Yeah, you know in my astral body. They could definitely see me, and it scared the heck out of them. Most of them thought I was some devil worshiper anyway. They got real afraid of me. Not all of them of course, I had a small number of friends maybe seven or eight."

"The second part of the plan was that I always tried to arrive at breakfast somewhat late. You know when everyone was about done. There were a number of uncovered wooden steps going up to the dinning area. They always kept the door closed at the top. When I walked up the stairs, I tried to make it loud as possible, especially the last few steps. Before I got to the top I could hear many of the chairs being pushed back from the table. When I entered the room it was cleared out except for only a few. My friends had a little smile on their faces, but not Yogananda. He was on to me from the start. He would gently chastise me. However, he would also allow me to ask questions and he answered them all, sometimes in detail."

"I always had questions, so I would wait awhile and then I would do it again. He never got real mad at me he would just say it was wrong. Maybe it was because my questions were important to me and I was sincere in my asking."

"Yogananda was very interested in the Pennsylvania Dutch magic that I knew about. I showed him everything that I had been taught. There was one time when it came in handy."

"There were two students of his that didn't like each other. They would always get into spats and this, in turn, would disturb the others. One was male, the other female. So Yogananda and I decided that we would try an experiment to see if the magic would end their constant fighting. I knew that this particular magic worked. I think Yogananda wanted to see if it worked and also and what would be the outcome."

"What was the magic," I asked with pronounced curiosity.

"It was the love binding magic. It casts a spell on both of the people and they are irresistibility draw to each other. To make it work you first need a few hairs from the man and the woman. You twist them together along with a certain ritual, and the magic starts."

"We managed to get the hairs from each, and with Yogananda's O.K., I set the magic in motion."

"They right away stopped their arguing. Then they started pleasantly talking to each other for longer and longer periods of time. Soon she baked a loaf of bread for him. They were becoming pretty good friends. Then someone saw them walking on the beach at night and holding hands."

"As soon as Yogananda heard this, he told me to end the magic because it was about to go too far. We accomplished what we had set out to do, and basically it was a good outcome for all concerned."

"In spite of this, Yogananda still had other ideas about the possible uses."

"One time when I was speaking with him semi-privately he reached into his pocket and pulled out some hairs. He asked me if I knew where they came from. I told him I had no idea where they came from. Then with a mischievous gleam in his eyes he proceeded to tell me that they came from the donkey he had on the land there. Then without much more of a warning, he quickly reached over toward my head. I ducked real fast and he missed his target, which was my hair. I moved away from him. I looked at him to try and get a sign of his intentions, but he still had this rather strange smile. I knew he was joking but I did not know how far he was willing to carry the joke. I think he wanted to see if there could be an attraction between the donkey and myself."

"So what happened?" I asked.

63

"He tried a few times to quickly approach me when I wasn't looking. He did this for about a week or so, and then he dropped it. I could see the humor of the whole thing, but I was too much a part of it at the time to think it was really funny."

"I see what you mean about his strange sense of humor. Do you think he was also teasing you a little?" I asked.

"Oh sure, that was part of the fun for him. He wanted to keep me guessing if he was serious or not."

"As I told you he was quite the host. He would entertain any number of world leaders. I don't know how he did it but many dignitaries always came to see him."

"He tried to be a positive influence on the world scene. He would make subtle suggestions and generally be an agent of good will."

"On a few occasions I got to meet some of these potentates. I told Yogananda that these world rulers did not leave any lasting impression on me. They seemed to be crude, shallow and vain."

"Yogananda explained that now I also knew why the world was in such a difficult state of affairs. He added that it was a pathetic situation."

"He asked me to come live at the Ashram. I was there when World War II started. We all used to sit up there on the cliffs overlooking the ocean, Yogananda included. You could see out to about five miles or more. You could see the ships burning from being hit by Japanese torpedos. They didn't say anything about it in the newspapers. The planes flew right over the temple. They said they used the golden lotus as the land marker indicating they should then turn out to sea. Later on the army made Yogananda put camouflage over it because the Japanese submarines used it as a marker too. Everyone noticed that the planes were loaded with bombs when they flew over us. They flew in groups of seven but they came back in threes and fours. Most of the bombs were gone and you could see holes in parts of them. This went on for days and days. Yogananda used to look through his telescope. One time he was looking at one of our destroyers going by close to shore. The telescope must have looked like a gun because they wheeled their cannon toward us. Quickly Yogananda told us to take the telescope away."

Shelly was laughing, and so was I. The danger of the situation had a comical appeal.

"Shelly, I know that you have enemies, and Yogananda did have them too?"

"Yes, of course, and its difficult to stay in balanced awareness 24 hours a day for protection. But he also had a very powerful magical amulet that Sri Yutiswar gave him. It had seven jewels set in gold and he wore it around his neck or arm 24 hours a day. The first time I saw it, I noticed it was tied by kite string. I told Yogananda that; "anyone could just take that from you." He said, "They could, but it would not do them any good. It was made for me alone". One of the main stones was a raw flat diamond with no facets. In fact all the stones were ground flat. You see they were used for their magical properties and not for their looks. The band was somewhat flexible and there were no inscriptions. Sri Yutiswar designed it himself, but I don't know who actually made it."

"The demons were trying to kill him by stopping his heart. Yogananda told me they would say, "See we have stopped your heart." Then Yogananda would say to them "O.K., well I can start my heart," and he did. This is why the amulet was made in the first place.

Putting myself in his place, I had to ask. "Was it hard to leave, Shelly?"

"I knew that I had to at some point. I had learned a great deal but it came time to go. I had one last, private meeting with him. I guess the disciples felt that I was in there too long with him. They started out by asking if everything was all right at the door, then they started yelling. By the time I left, they were threatening to break the door down."

I was quite shocked by this statement, but when I thought about all the immature emotions and their possessiveness it made sense to me.

In an air of concluding things Shelly made a revealing statement.

"He was a real Master of this I have no doubt. But he could be surprisingly humble about it. I once asked him what does his first name Paramahansa mean. He said" If we are to go from here to the ends of the universe, then I have only gone one inch!"

"We stayed in contact with each other in a spiritual and symbolic way. He was in my dreams fairly often. He was here physically another nine years. Even after he left his body we stayed in contact, but it was more abstract. This is because when he was in a completely balanced state he was shielded so nobody would know where he was. How could they, when he is like that he occupies no time or position in space. When he comes out of that state, then you can find him and he can find you."

"By seeing the Atma (immortal Spirit) in all beings, and all beings in the Atma you go to Brahman (God), this is the only way."

—Kaivalya-Upanishad

"Love without end, has no end"

—Proverb

CHAPTER 6.

KNOWING KRIYA

I had been teaching Kriya Yoga and astrology in Boulder and Denver Colorado since 1970. By the grace of the Gurus and my own drug free stance I somehow survived. My major habit was meditation. It saved me from many karmic predicaments time and time again. It also protected me from the never-ending, uncompromising emotional turmoil of the everyday world.

Shelly's perfect demeanor and cool delivery remained a constant on all my visits. Even when Majorie departed this world and the dog died he was as smooth as ever. The iron fist of his undaunted will was ever present. I longed for his brand of straightforward wisdom. They were the surprising insights that come from a mystery-hunting mind.

$$*\qquad*\qquad*$$

"Shelly you said that Kriya means; I am Aware that I am."

"That's right, it's the Self Realizing itself over and over again, and being blissfully aware in the process."

"The techniques of Kriya Yoga are based on proven scientific formulas. The special breaths go directly to the flow of currents in the spine. The techniques have come down to us from India and ancient Egypt. It is true that Kriya deals with a number of abstract concepts that are not easily interpreted."

Yogananda would always say that it was not necessary to believe in Kriya. He said that the technique was not based on beliefs or disbeliefs. Anyone who does it correctly will get the same results. That's what I mean when I say it is scientific. You know going to outer space is expensive, but with Kriya, anyone willing can journey to the vastness of inner space."

I could tell he was going to take the conversation some place, but neither one of us knew where.

"Look, if A+B=C, and also Y+X=Z, and if A and B are good and Y and X are bad; then why do most people want to think bad about others?"

I decided to take a shot at.

"Because the greater emphasis in this world is on Z?"

He did not acknowledge my statement one way or another.

"It's because people have untrained and undisciplined minds. They are emotionally conditioned early on. They usually pick up a lot of adversity from their parents. Then sooner or later they get hurt, so then they want to hurt others."

"You know they have tried to sell newspapers that concentrated primarily on good things. They all went bankrupt. People are emotionally fixated. If they get a strong enough stimulus from an aspect in their charts, then their desires and emotions get stirred up and they no longer care if their actions are right or wrong."

"Only if you are able to think in a calm and abstract way, does it offer you the possibility to be objective about situations."

I silently said, "Yes."

"Emotions are not on the level of actions when you are in meditation. They are quieted down. We know this because there is a ratio of 4 to 1. This is the heartbeat to breath ratio, after a person has been meditating for a while. Often it starts out as 8 heart beats per Kriyic breath. On average it takes about 20 to 30 seconds per Kriya. Your intake of oxygen will decrease over time. Your brain and body slowly becomes saturated with oxygen and with the subtle pranic energy. As the heart rate decreases so does the breathing. The heart is then allowed to rest. Then the thinking process also calms down. So, this is why they call shamadi or deep Yogic trance the "breathless state.""

"Many singers and horn players have a certain control over their breathing. The techniques in Hatha Yoga and certain pranayamas (that is regulated breathing) are also very beneficial."

"The actual amount of oxygen that a person can take in depends on the capacity of their lungs. A person born with either Aires or Scorpio as an ascendant can have a lung capacity holding as much as

700cc of air. People with Gemini or Virgo rising can have a much smaller capacity of 250cc on average. The larger capacity gives those people a stronger endurance."

"Find a friend with a large lung capacity and see if you can keep up with them, he added."

"The Kriyic breath also decarbonizes the blood as well as removing other impurities. Yogananda had doctors check his blood before and after he meditated. There was always less carbon in the blood. I don't know if they checked for a weight loss.

"So will these large lunged people have stronger Kriyas?" I asked.

"Not necessarily but they will be able to store more energy in their system. Remember, it's: duration times intensity. The focused mental intensity varies from person to person. So lung capacity is secondary to a dedicated and devotional practitioner."

"Many students get caught up in the numbers game. It's the strength of each and every Kriya, not how many you can do. There is no race here. It should be a pleasurable experience. Meditation is really the; "effortless control of the awareness."

"Yes, Shelly I remember you saying that. So some people may never get to 108 Kriyas per day?"

"That's right, the fact is they may not need to do that many."

"Don't forget that Kriya is accelerating the natural currents that happen annually. There is a very minor solar and lunar current that happens every day and another every solar and lunar month. The main current happens in about 12 months. When you breath Kriya, you are in fact moving the energy through your own internalized solar system. You are actually reversing the direction of nature's currents and breathing as God does.

Therefore symbolically, and actually, one Kriya breath is equal to a whole year of living. It of course does not start out that way. You will, at you own pace begin to awaken from what could be described as a hypnotic sleep. With continued practice your progress will eventually accelerate. Then it will increase to the point where each breath is equal to a number of years. It can go to three years, then 7 years, then 21 years, and onward."

"Under what they call "normal conditions," it would take a person 10 million years to reach God consciousness. Two million years, if you don't count the time between each life and early childhood!"

"Kriya takes you off your astrological chart, or as they say the wheel of suffering. It balances out all the aspectual angles. It gets you off the cross of matter and into the center of the chart, the center that is balanced. Remember the chart is the not-Self, it's a bunch of things."

"You can see quite easily how a person is programmed by analyzing their astrological chart. It's what makes people act like robots. It's a huge mix of thoughts and emotions that must be overcome to realize the Self."

"All the karma is in either the Ida or Pingalic spinal currents, (left lunar and right solar). The central susamonic awareness eventually balances out all karma. Karma can't function in that middle bliss current."

"I have told a number of people that when they become more balanced they will naturally loose interest in many things of this world, even sex. Then I heard that about twenty of them stopped their Kriya practice because they felt it would interfere with their sex life!"

A broad smile appeared on his face but it did not turn to laughter this time.

"If you keep meditating, a simplified version of the laws of existence begins to become evident in your life. These laws we are discussing are applicable anywhere in God's cosmic dream. So you can see that under these circumstances Kriya is the solver of all problems. It will evidentially explain them all and then neutralize them."

"I understand Shelly, but it does take a certain amount time for things to happen."

"Yes it does take number of years but this is a really small amount of time when you consider the many thousands of years most people have been trapped in the cycle of reincarnation."

"At some point you will become 51% awareness of the Self. Then you will be more able to communicate this to those that are interested. Of course the ones who are supposedly interested always have a right to think any way they want. While at the same time major ideas in society and their own karma are influencing them. You can bring a horse to water, but you can't make it drink."

"I ask you how much did they really listen to Christ or Buddha?"

He was so "right there" with this statement. People hear what they want to hear.

"I can tell you this; a saint or sage is the last person to know it. It all has to do with the equilibrium of balance. A person who is advanced along these lines is acutely aware of any and all imbalances and imperfections they may have. Because of this, they never feel that they are in the lofty place that others may see them in."

"You should know that eventually everyone finds their way through the maze of Self. One of the reasons is that it's already contained within the memory track of God. We are dreaming our limited dreams, within his dream. All time, space and every event is here right now. So all pathways lead to God, even the strangest and darkest ones."

I could not let this one go by.

"Yes, Shelly, but there are some horrorable pathways out there."

"Yes, that's true, there are some I would definitely avoid at all costs. But you see this is only our opinion and therefore it's not really objective at all. How do we know what a particular being really needs in order to grow spiritually?"

"So what's the difference between any being, and God? God is balanced Self Conscious Awareness, which is ever-new bliss. We are unbalanced and mostly unaware. We are in the image of God but still caught in the maze of our own making. We are certainly not in a blissful state most of the time. Therefore, the external conditions are a direct reflection of our inner state."

"Keep in mind that there are a heck of a lot of disturbing equations in trying to live a spiritual life. People need to start asking questions. Hopefully the Kriya breath will stimulate people to do so."

"One of the reasons why we meditate is to open our minds to new concepts that are just beyond our present perceptions. We meditate to reclaim ourselves.

"You could look at it this way; susamonic current IS balanced being, and cosmic consciousness is the understanding of that balanced being." Right now you can observe any or all things in this room. But in God consciousness you are all things observing you!

Now what we have been discussing are ideas related to direct Kriya, but remember there is indirect Kriya. Many activities can cause the Kriyic current to flow in the spine. Let me just say that teaching is the strongest form of indirect Kriya. Teaching others spiritual things has allowed many to reach God Consciousness. You are helping others and so you must be self-sacrificing; this causes tremendous growth."

I took great solace in his words; I began to realize that living ones life in the world and being on the path are one and the same.

"Shelly, you have said that the lineage of Kriya teachers are really only concerned with meditation. They like to keep the material things of life very simple."

"Yes, that's right. Yogananda said to me, "When you can meditate as easily on a five dollar chair as on a fifty thousand dollar one then you have mastered meditation. Then he went right over and sat in the most comfortable chair he could find."

When he was completing the last part of his sentence his chest started to heave with what burst into uncontrolled laughter.

He moved a little in a different direction, and continued to speak.

"There are a number of very subtle things that can aid our understanding. For example our awareness is affected by inner sounds happening after continuous practice. These audible and inaudible sounds are part of the techniques of the Kriyic breath. The currents play the main musical instrument of your body, which is your cerebral spinal system."

"In the past man abused the power of sound. So there is a lot of confusion about it. We can't get a completely clear idea of how certain sounds effect specific spinal centers. At this time in the world we are in the process of finding this all out again."

"Do you think we will find the answers, Shelly?" I asked hopefully.

"I once did some calculations and I found there was not enough time with the number of meditators at hand to try all the possible sounds. Anyway, the Kriyic sounds are a very good approximation."

"You know that there are basically six major variations of the Kriyic breath. For most practioners it is usually not required that they do all of them. But Yogananda said there are literally thousands of minor and major variations."

He then quickly added, "Don't forget the three second silent pause at the Sun/Son center. What you hold in your mind at that place will begin to manifest in your world"

A mild panic ran through me, so I asked, "Shelly I usually don't think of anything."

"That is alright," was his consoling answer.

"But Shelly, the Yoga books that I have read indicate that you should concentrate on the Lord only, or your chosen deity as a representation of God."

"That's O.K. to do, if you want," was his assuring answer.

Then from some unknown place he fired a warning at me.

"You can't make progress by using the solar plexus energy. This type of physical force will only increase the heart rate. The process has to be effortless, or as close to it as possible. Just be aware, it's your awareness that controls the brain's thinking, not the other way around."

"It's also not good to do the major Kriya when you are angry. The gut level is again over activated with intense emotions."

"Also it is recommended that during the woman's monthly cycle, or if you are really sick, then the major Kriya should be temporarily avoided. Under all of these circumstances you can still do the mental Kriya, (by observing the natural breathing through the nose), if you want, just don't push it."

*   *   *

I had settled into a certain amount of comfortable assurance. Did I actually understand what he was saying? It wasn't going to last very long. I had no idea about the shallowness of my perception. In the coming sessions there would be many times that I could almost hear my brain cells popping. Not to mention the profound humility that comes with wondering about the unlimited and vast possibilities in God's dream.

I had been experiencing another evening in Shelly's timeless world. I found it remarkably easy to pretend that the rest of the world did not exist. I actually believed it didn't when I was with him. How often did I bath in the silent splendor of his "presence"?

"The Kriyic current sets up a harmonic wave pattern within the 360 degree circle. The fundamental wave sounds start at zero degrees or one. Then it moves to the second harmonic, which is 180 degrees, then 3 or 120 degrees, and it goes through all the possible harmonics. This is why no two states of awareness are the same."

"As I mentioned before, we lost most of the "laws of sound". It was about 11,500 years ago. Later on the "Tower of Babble" was an attempt to psychically reconstruct the lost laws, but it failed."

"However we still can hear the subtle sounds from each of the centers. The Sun and Moon centers in the head make no sound, or you could say the stillness within all sound; which is AUM (OM). The Mercury/cervical center is the sound of the ocean roar. The Venus/cardiac center has the sound of bells. You can really hear this when you are in love. The rest of the centers don't have that distinct of a sound."

"In the Mars/solar plexus you can create heat, you could even start a fire and then reverse it and put it out. The Jupiter/sacral plexus is the element of water; complete control of that center, for example, would allow you to walk on water. The Saturn center at the tip of the spine connects us to the earth and to inner earth."

"I have mentioned the three spinal currents; Ida the left/Lunar, Pingalic right/Solar and the middle, balanced Susamonic current. When you look at a person's chart it tells you about all the imbalances or karma, but almost nothing about real spirituality. It shows you both imbalances of Ida and Pingala because they are still on the wheel of cause and effect.

Each of the six centers has their own polarity, (2x6) which equals 12. This is where we get the Kriyic twelve letter mantra sounds. Six sounds to the left and six to the right. As you know each person's centers can be understood by looking at the houses in their horoscope. (See Chapter 9.)

"The Pingalic side is like a positive charged electron or odd number, and Ida is like negativity charged proton or an even number. When you times +X and -X, then the answer is Zero. The susamonic current is like a zero, and therefore not on the chart. You could say it's in the center or void. In that state you feel a peace that is before (surpasses) all understanding and a bliss that pours forth over your whole being."

"Even some of the psychic powers are in a state of imbalance. Powers are part of our desire nature. Anything that produces imbalances over a period of time is basically considered evil. Yet hate, as well as the love of God, can act as a driving forces of attraction because they both can be 180 degrees out of phase."

"True spirituality is about entering the bliss state. Blissful meditation is the result of taking the middle path. The right and left hand paths will karmically crucify a person in a variety of ways."

Shelly, you are saying that the balanced susamonic state it is formless?

"Yes, there is no form or dimensions there. Tell me what is the weight of unselfish love? What's its atomic number? Why can't you tell me these measurements? Can you tell me the measurements of a toothache?"

I kept saying, "No, I can't" in a semi audible mumble to let him know that I was trying to understand.

"There is no form there, and therefore to some it may appear to have no meaning."

But Shelly, you told me once that there were beings in there.

"Yes, there are, but they are in a state of balanced awareness. They are not in space or time, because those are dimensions. They are in fact everywhere and nowhere, which is a paradox, and perhaps the best way to express it."

Then he added quickly, "Now, when you are in God Consciousness you are in all states simultaneously!"

I took a slow deep breath.

"When doing major Kriya we visualize the rising cool current going through the center of the whole spine starting at the tip or tail. Then see the warm current descending from the Sun center and over

75

the head. While staying a little above or outside the spine. It's very important to psychically feel the warmth and coolness, if you can."

It seemed like I was learning the basics in Kriya and Buddhistic physics. I tried to enjoy it as much as I could.

"Many beings are way out of balance, yet God allows them to exist within his balanced dream. That's because of his unselfish love, and the fact that all life forms have a degree of Self-Conscious Awareness. But at some point we have to move from just being an image of God, to experiencing God."

"Look," he said bluntly, "even a cockroach can survive radiation, as well as the great variations of temperature and pressure."

"The right pingalic current is in the lower dimensions or the physical. It is immense because it's from here to the Quasars. The left current or Ida is the world of sleep. In that state, or the astral plane, you can access to higher dimensions, but there are limitations in doing so."

"The Kriya is continuously lifting the energy from the three lower centers to the three higher centers. These currents are always active and sometimes they can cause blockages or eddies in the spine. This is why it is so important that the teacher listen to the person's Kriyic breath. Then if necessary, you can run your fingers slowly across the certain spinal sections. You can feel where the problems are located. Gently massaging the area in a circular motion, while sending out the healing Kriyic current can be a helpful."

I thought to myself, "You are beginning to learn that the only real strength we have comes through the self-discipline of meditation. In that practice we can at last attain the unlimited state of balanced Self-Conscious Awareness."

"The process is fairly simple. You are the meditator or Self and the observer. Then there is the act of meditating and observing. This act is observing the object of meditation or the not self. When all three merge you have one perfect meditation. (See Appendix A.)

"I want you to visualize holding a pendulum at your third eye."

"Like holding it from my forehead?

"Yes, this pendulum can swing in both extremes of left and right, or it can be centered. You control the swing whether you know it or not. Do you want to have large or small swings? Do you want to create a short or long path for your Self?"

"Well, I don't want large swings," was my answer.

"Yes, that's right, you want the minimum amount of swing." He then remained silent, allowing me to ponder.

"However, when you do create, it's usually in pairs; when there's a proton, there has to be an anti-proton. So in creation there is always duality."

"Now remember, you don't want to think about any of these ideas I've mentioned when actually practicing Kriya. Leave the psychology and philosophy for discussions only. You have been told how to picture the current flowing in the spine. This is what you visualize. Of course, there are many subtle things going on, but you should not focus on them while you are in meditation."

All I could muster was an affirmative, "Yes."

I then had to plea my case. "Shelly, my mind is always filled with so many thoughts."

"So what," was his quick answer.

"That's what the brain does. It thinks more then it needs to. These thoughts are like little children who are seeking your attention. You need to dismiss them gently. Tell yourself that you will deal with these thoughts, emotions or problems later."

"Keep your spine straight, slightly contract the stomach and anus muscles, eyes gently focused above the eyebrows, the chin even with the floor, and the palms up. Don't forget that the meditation area should be as free as possible from noise and distractions. The place or room where you meditate in should be only for that purpose, if possible. Sitting on wool covered by silk is best. You can face either East or North. Also, before you start, doing some Hatha Yoga or even a few simple stretches is always helpful."

"As you continue to meditate, all thoughts will begin to exercise less and less control. Also there will be less emotion behind them. They will become more and more an activity that is only on the surface. The greater part of your awareness will not be connected to them. You will find yourself just observing them, and this is because the whole body and mind has quieted down. Then one day you will become aware that there is a complete absence of thought."

I begin to feel pretty good after his statements, but it only lasted a brief moment.

Then he hit me with one of the most deeply penetrating statements of the evening.

"Do you want to be in control, or do you want to continue on and be controlled?"

He really had put his finger on a sore spot within my soul. Ever since I could remember I had the feeling, notion and consistent perception of being controlled. It was usually a little different then the basic issues within parental and authority conflicts. It was more like a profound and deep sense of "being messed with" in a very hidden way. It had been there from my earliest memories. It didn't make me an unnecessarily paranoid person, or a rebel without a clue. But non-the-less, it was always in the back of my mind. Somebody or something had, was, and did try to continue to manipulate and adversely influence my thoughts and actions. I never wanted them to have the upper hand whoever or whatever they were. The ability to be completely free of any and all external control is what I yearned for, and naturally it dominated my intentions.

"Shelly, you said that one of the basic concerns of the Kriya lineage of teachers is how certain practical things effect your ability to meditate. Like if your house is warm and cool when necessary, and if you have enough to eat."

"Yes, they are primarily concerned with the basics of life. They know when the fundamental needs are met; a person will be inclined to meditate. I mean what do you actually need? According to them not very much."

Shelly continued on what seemed to be the theme of the day.

"The Kriyic current moves through the centers in many ways. Yogananda said there were many minor centers, but basically only six. I know many of the books talk about seven, but the Sun and Moon in the head center really act as one. The frontal cortex or Sun center is the Christ or Krishna consciousness. The medulla area in back of the head is the Moon center, often called the mouth of God. It is the place of God consciousness when it interacts with the Sun. Working together they open the 1000 petaled lotus at the top of the head. This is why Yogananda said that in order to activate the top of the head, concentrate on the Sun center. Then he would often quote the bible by saying; "no one can get to the Father except through the Sun/Son."

"The interesting thing is nobody can really motivate or force another to meditate; it has to come from within the person. Each person must decide that it is important for survival, or it is not. We have a programmed feeling complex within us that blocks the awareness of the true Self. When one overcomes this complex, then progress can be quite rapid.

"Only in deep meditation can you overcome the powerful influences of the body, the breath, heart and the brain. All will calm down considerably. Then everything becomes crystal clear. This causes your knowledge to digest into wisdom.

"You should begin to see how your childhood emotional patterns dominate your life. We are all emotional children. Maturity in that area is usually set before five years of age."

"The important point is that meditation will allow you to make significant decisions from an unemotional and relatively quiet and objective mind. Now that's the real power, because eventually you can then "will" something to happen in deep meditation, and it actually happens."

Also when you meditate you indirectly help all others on the planet. If a Yogi went into God-Consciousness in the forest he or she would naturally lift all mankind just a little. If one's wife meditates she helps her husband and in turn they both lift the whole family.

"So continue to set aside a time and place to meditate. Make sure you are comfortably still. If you feel some uncomfortable strain you are doing something wrong."

"Turn your gaze completely inward and focus on the third eye. Meditate like there is no tomorrow. But most important of all build and build on the enjoyment until it is a permanent habit. We all like repeating what we find enjoyable."

...and so Ajuna become a Yogi...

—Bhagavad Gita

CHAPTER 7.

HERE, THERE, AND EVERYWHERE

I could describe my meetings with Shelly as a series of performances. Certainly not in the theoretical sense, like he purposely staged them. They were, however, quite dramatic, completely entertaining, and always provocative.

Each and every session was a special blessing. It seemed like it was designed and carried out for some future person at some future date. It was a sublime teaching not only in content, but also in delivery. Something wonderful, sacred and unimaginable was always just beyond the range of my conscious knowing, and just slightly out of reach of what is explainable.

He was definitely keeping it simple for me, but at the same time it was building toward some, as yet, unknown premise. It was going to be some kind of shocking news or unexpected insight, I thought. I just had to hang in there, and not jump in "somehow," when I knew full well, that I was over my head. I was learning and remembering, but I felt it was at a pitifully slow pace.

As usual, Shelly just spontaneously began to talk as if the questions were asked, and in a way that disregarded any interlude of time since we last met.

"Wherever your center of awareness is, that is where you place your values. As you develop spiritually, different things become important. You begin to have a number of new attitudes about your Self. Eventually Self-Realization makes you live by an entirely different code. You see things from a new vantage point."

"Because of all these changes in your awareness you realize that you can't really judge another, nor can they judge you. You simply no longer obey any standards, whether they come from a genius or a moron.

"Objective and subjective reality have changed for the mystic. The subjective awareness is now the interpreter of the objective reality. Physical beauty may still be skin deep, but the eye of the beholder is no longer stuck in the ego."

"For the average person, simple reality exists as factors of having outer and inner parts, and it's your skin that separates these two worlds. It is the largest organ of the body, that's why it is said that the soul of a person resides in the skin."

"A number of people look at a painting which is some person's impression of reality. After they look, then they get their very own impression of reality. Likewise, two lovers looking at a waterfall see it in a completely different way then a scientist standing next to them.

By now I was puzzled. "What was he getting at?" I thought.

"God is trying to teach us, but we busy dreaming about reality instead of seeing reality as the dream that it is. Even the truth is a relative reality."

"The simple fact is, people are attuned to the symbolic nature of the reality they have chosen to be relative too. You could say they have a sympathetic connection on a sub-conscious level. This is why sympathetic magic works. Just like the symbols of astrology they both effect the sub-conscious mind."

Before I could ask him to expand on this point he continued on.

"No one has to be taught to think symbolically. Psychologists have seen it in the children all over the world."

"Your basic forces take on a symbolic nature in dreams. For example, it is always a good omen to move upward in a dream. This is because you are moving away from gravity. If you are moving downward you are symbolically fall back into a gravity world."

"Dreams are trying to tell you about the future by creating a symbolic story. If you have enough awareness in that state you can understand the symbolism and you can change it. When you can do this repeatedly, you have, in fact changed your future!"

Changing the symbols changes the future events. He said it in such a nonchalant way that I could have easily missed it.

"Another point is that all force fields are symbolized by entities real and imaginary. You want to see them before they see you. Therefore you need to study your dreams. You need to understand the

81

laws of symbolic association and how they work for you. Otherwise it's like you are cast adrift in the middle of the ocean trying to find your way.

Then he quickly added, "We are all trying to find our way in God's cosmic dream."

"Dreams are in the world of Ida, the left Lunar current. When you can no longer hold on to the balanced current you begin to dream or you are in the awake state."

"Most people have a tendency to move too quickly from the awake state to the dream state, then they rapidly by-pass the balanced state. Meditation will allow you to enter the dream world and the balanced state more consciously.

"Shelly, you just said that entities are symbolic of force fields."

"Yes, that's right. The force fields in God's dream are both positive and negative. Positive and negative in time, space and matter.

At that time I lacked the ability to put forth a good follow-up question, so I just remained silent.

"It's a dream, a cosmic drama that we live in, so enjoy it as much as you can. We are all actors on the stage as they say. That's why I like to play my part to the fullest, while remaining in control. As I told you, Yogananda played his part to the hilt."

I didn't want to whine, but it was easy for him to say. I still felt very caught in the illusionary nature of life. Yet, I did realize that he wasn't saying that I had to renounce the world. Rather I was to enjoy it while at the same time renouncing it within myself. It was a tall order, but one that was in direct alignment with a Kriya Yogi's embracing the householder lifestyle.

After a very brief pause, Shelly started speaking again.

"Steve, you have to learn to get over your selfish impulses. Learn to give of yourself. Give more then you think you can give. You can provide a spiritual service as an act of giving. The greatest thing that a person can give is knowledge and information."

"This is why teaching is the greatest form of giving. It's the best type of service possible. It is the most powerful form of indirect Kriya. Even if you teach with attachment, it is still helpful."

"So, when you are sacrificing yourself for others (instead of the other way around) you are really receiving back from others. What you do unto another you are doing to your self."

As usual, he anticipated my question before I asked it.

"When you teach others about spiritual things, the Kriyic current will automatically flow in your spine. It is not as powerful as actually breathing Kriya, that's why we call it indirect. The idea is that you are both growing together."

When he answered my questions like this, I knew his views about the nature of my mind had to be remarkable. I also knew that he was amused with the whole process. He often broke out into hysterical laughter when talking about my behavior. However, he was very good-natured about it, never did it seem demeaning or mean.

Early in our relationship he had asked for permission to enter into my mind. There wasn't any sinister implications implied, nor did I feel invaded or continuously under the microscope. It was just that he needed to know my mental and emotional patterns, as he called them. Evidentally there was a lot of rearranging that had to take place.

Shelly kept tying the pieces together.

"When a person enters a particular path, the real question is: how much free will do I actually have on this path?"

"Most organized religions say that they are teaching spirituality but it is a big let down when you want to go deeper. Religion is incredibly emotional, I wonder sometimes if people are using their minds at all. They say the same old stuff over and over again."

"It's no wonder that almost all the wars that have been fought have been over God. Don't you find this ironic? People are not supposed to kill each other, but they really enjoy doing so when it's over their concepts about God."

"In the Middle Ages the high priests of the churches could not satisfy the curiosity of the people. The educated people begin asking very different questions. The type of questions that were asked produced the beginnings of the scientific age."

"Before this time, people thought about the world in primitive ways. Many thought that Atlas, an elephant or a turtle held up a flat world. You probably know the rest of what happened."

"Now here is another point. How could God have created you? That would imply that you had a beginning and therefore you would have an end. You are immortal now and forever, without beginning and end. God has no beginning or end, and you are in the image of God, aren't you? As I have told you, the only difference is the degrees of Self-Conscious Awareness."

"So we are Gods in the making, living within the creation of this cosmic dreamer, the one we call God, I mused.

I figured I should have had a few more moments to digest his statements, but it was not in the plan for that evening.

"Remember that the concept of God is a paradox. If you actually could explain God then you also could explain him away. When you explain him, you restrict him, God is unrestricted and can't really be explained. Now, if you speak in a symbolic way using abstract concepts, you can convey a somewhat limited view of the Cosmic Dreamer.

"So, God is like a Zen koan. If you think you can explain him, it's not Zen. This is very similar to the uncertainty principle in physics. You think that you can measure the mass of an electron, and when you do so, you instantly infer and change its speed. But do you really know where it is and how much speed it has?"

"We have the same problems in the mystical areas don't we? What solid proof do you have of your past lives? How can you convince another that you had a dream? So you see, there is a big difference between believing something and knowing something.

"The particular statement that I like is; "God is a circumference, whose center is everywhere. This center is infinite pi and therefore infinite in energy"

"Unfortunately most people are far from understanding God, when their brains are continually immersed in glandular secretions. The basic life form that you really are is not at home on a planet, it's real home is deep space. That's why gravity worlds are "veils of tears". Look at us; our organs, they are on the exterior of our bodies. It's not supposed to be like that, everything should be contained within a sphere of light.

"When the current in your spine is fully above the cervical center, you can't explain anything anyway; it's because you can't speak. You literally cannot function like normal when your consciousness is in the head centers. In the beginning you may have an idea that you can, but you will find out that the current must shift to the left or right and drop to the neck."

"Shelly, what if a person is in cosmic consciousness?"

"Then that person is in all the planes at the same time. Like Yogananda said, "You are a distinct wave in an ocean of infinite consciousness."

His statement gave my mind a needed twist. At least it gave me an original idea of a state of awareness that was remote from my experiential point of view.

After all, I thought, the Yogis were always saying, "why wait?" You don't have to pretend or just talk about the ultimate reality. By doing this and that technique in the correct way over a period of time, the result is that you can experience for yourself the vastness of cosmic consciousness.

Shelly had said a number of times that the whole endeavor was really simple, but it just looked complex. He explained that it does no good to get over-eager for the end results. His emphasis was that it was always better in continuing to enjoy the process.

All I knew was that I had been receiving his expert coaching, so essentially there were unlimited possibilities. It was especially comforting to know that he was continuously looking out for me. It almost goes without saying; that I was not always conscious of his all-encompassing guardianship.

Bringing things into perspective, he started to speak again.

"No matter what experiences you may have, you should remain true to yourself. Be your natural self, and by saying this, I mean you should be the best of who you are. You can't really be other then who you are anyway. Sure, your personality has limitations, so work on them. You have made some improvements, and I know you can continue doing so."

This was one of the rare moments that he actually gave me a compliment. He would never say it was so, but rather that he was stating a simple fact.

"Look at me, at this point in my life I still should get a little exercise. But I don't do it. I do think Hatha Yoga is fine but I have never practiced it. As a joke, some of the people at the Chicago Temple sent me a diploma in Hatha Yoga.

"Yogananda highly recommended physical exercise. But at the time I was with him he didn't need, or want to do very much. I used to see him in the morning, just looking at his swimming pool, rarely did he swim in it."

"Christ was true to his nature, when he got very angry and threw the money changers out of the Temple. They watered it down a little by calling it "righteous indignation".

"However, many times personality problems can really get in the way of spiritual teachings. This is why it was said that: "No man can be a prophet in his own land." This isn't exactly true because Mohammed was a great prophet and it was in his own land. His first convert was his wife, and you know that a woman knows all about a husband's imperfections."

I thought to myself. "It may be irrational but most people don't want a real teacher with any personality problems. What they seen to want are close encounters with non-humans or angels or at least someone they can emotionally idealize."

Shelly continued, "It's typical that they just can't believe that the limitations of their psychological makeup has anything to do with their perceptions of others. Alter all, the point for them is, that the teacher is not quite Godly or perfect enough for them.

"We all have concepts about ourselves, some are true, and others are not. In my case, I strongly feel that I was an accomplished military leader in a past life, not on this earth. So I have from a certain point of view, a completely irrational idea that I am a great military genius. If I see some conflict in the world going on, I think I have the answers. Even when I was little I would immediately protest against certain lessons in school. I was always arguing with my teachers about one thing or another." One of them was so upset with me he said, "Burning at the stake has been stopped but in your case Shelly maybe we can make an exception!"

"I am not what I am because I want to be that way. I am what I am because I have no choice in the matter whatsoever. It isn't a case of what I want or don't want!

I really wasn't ready for this provocative statement. It really left me quite puzzled and somewhat confused. Where was the free will we are all supposed to have? I did not feel at that time that any questioning was proper. The process had an amazing way of pushing answers into the future.

"You see, I consider military actions as a very high and perfect art form. I realize to most people that this sounds a little crazy, but I enjoy the complex strategy immensely.

All these admissions kind of stunned me. It didn't take long for a deep feeling of devotion and gratitude to well up within me. It was clear that he was telling me these things because we had finally established a friendship. I was being temporarily welcomed into his clan, army, and spiritual family. A preliminary level of trust had been reached. I was somewhat nervous about screwing it up.

While playing with his lighter his face registered a fond memory.

"This particular spiritual disposition may have helped me when I was drafted in WWII."

"Oh really, Shelly," I said, while being the picture of attentiveness.

"Like many other young men at the time I was required to go through a pre-draft physical. I was standing in line in my underwear with the other men. I struck up a conversation with a few of the men closest to me in line. One thing led to another and we started talking about spiritual things and the future. This one guy asked me to read his palm. This of course sparked the curiosity of others. Well, before you knew it, I had done a number of readings. I kept it brief but to the point. I remember telling a few of them that they could die in France, in a place called Normandy! After about a half-hour of this, the line of men were all talking loudly about what I had said. While others were demanding that I read their palms. An army officer was watching this whole drama unfold and he made a decision to pull me out of line. They took me to a room and started asking me what I was doing. I didn't hide anything; I just told them I was reading the future in their hands. They didn't know what to make of me except that I was causing a disruption to their orderly process. There were four officials and they all voted. They rejected me by a margin of 4 to 0.

One of them said, "We don't want your kind in the United States Army!" So that was the end of my military career."

He began laughing in a slow and deep manner.

I realized that he didn't want to be disruptive or cause any problems at the induction center. In fact he was more then ready to enter the military. But as it turned out, he was just being himself and it changed his destiny.

He began speaking again but in a more serious tone.

"This was one of the events that caused a major change in my life. Everyone needs these types of experiences that can alter their destiny. I'm sure that most people would agree with that idea. But when you take a look at their lives, it's a different matter."

"They all complain about their variety of problems quite a bit. Yet when it comes down to actually changing things, it's another story. Down here in Florida there are a lot of older people. They have a real preoccupation in complaining about their health. You hear one of them complaining about a health problem and the other will say. "Suffer, girl, you don't know what suffering is until.""

"I actually knew a husband and wife who were in competition with each other on who could have the most organs taken out. That is a true story."

"Then there are the people that build their house close to the river. The floods come and wipe them out. So what do they do? They go right back and build their house in the same way and in the same place only to be wiped out again. They will give you all kinds of reasons why, but it just doesn't make any sense. These type of sad events make the human condition a very disturbing prospect."

"Yogananda told me that he was happy that he did not have to be physical anywhere anymore. He said that his work would be in the astral worlds of light, close and far from this earth. He was no longer interested in having a physical body."

"Think about how your senses control you. For example your sight, and how it affects you thinking. How your fingers control your brain and how they are controlled by it. Being a humanoid almost completely controls your thinking process and your spiritual awareness. Then how you think about yourself controls how you think about others. This in turn will determine how they react to you."

"It's the blind leading the blind," I whispered.

Some could certainly say that Shelly took a dim view of human nature. I felt it was refreshingly realistic. He seemed to give words to many semi-conscious perceptions that I had over the years.

"I learned very early on in this life what you are learning now. That human beings are, on one level, machines that like to solve problems."

They have to solve many problems or else, was my silent thought.

"Now you are learning something very important."

"What am I learning?" I asked sensitively.

"You are learning one of best of all possible things. You are learning about how much you really don't know."

"A wise man knows a little something about all the things he doesn't really know. But a person who thinks they are brilliant doesn't know what they could know yet. They are still too enamored with themselves and their intellects."

I just sat quietly for a moment or two. Then I said that it was getting late. I didn't want to keep him up. Some of his guests would go on until two or three in the morning. I didn't want to abuse what I considered a sacred privilege.

Earlier that day I found a poem of his. It was just lying on the floor of his small workshop. I mentioned it to him and he acknowledged that he had written it some years ago, but he seemed strangely indifferent to its content and me finding it.

Before the beginning – chaos reigned in the infinities
Countenance beheld not countenance in balanced equilibrium
Creation followed creation in unsustained fury
Until one Brother held forth the vestments of honor
In his essence the maze of Self was solved
In Him – countenance beheld countenance in balanced glory
Bliss flowed forth in undulating waves of joy
The sustained spiral of creation hewed forth into being
The Brothers flocked to pay homage and obedience before the Master
The wave of bliss spread unto all willing
That they might sup of the nectar of crystalline dew

They descended into Him and moved about the pathways
To behold the law of the maze
Brother communicated unto brother the golden essence of truth
Countenance beheld countenance in the splendid visionage of balance
Brothers became lost in the maze
Others descended to lend aid
The sustained creation was maintained in balance
Against the folly of the fallen Brothers
Sustained creation shall remain sustained
Until all Brothers in infinity stand
Hallowed by the Blissful countenance of Balanced Being.

CHAPTER 8.

A BRIEF GLIMPSE OF TRUE SCIENCE

As time passed I suspected that Shelly was holding back, somewhat, on a number of subjects. I really can't speculate as to his real reasons, but that it seemed a necessary part of the whole process. During the following sessions he decided to express a sizable piece of his cosmological theology. Although he does not reach any ultimate conclusions, a plethora of seed ideas are presented for review and reflection.

Although Shelly's chunks of information were presented in a concise and logical manner, he did not always reveal where in the puzzle they should be placed. Therefore in this chapter I have attempted to put his theories and insights into a chronological order that shows the most complete picture possible. The following are his theoretical views.

"Some claim that I try and mix science and spiritual things. To tell you the truth I don't think that there is a big difference. I am interested in the basic truths of life, and so I will go wherever and whenever to get the answers. I have received information from what some would call very unorthodox places. The fact is that science has many answers to spiritual questions and vice versa. It's all in how you perceive the information. When you look at science in a spiritual way you can get some very valuable ideas. The only separation between the two goes on in people's heads."

"I have told you that all of the secret teachings are coded in symbols and numbers. Science has their symbols and numbers and so does the occult sciences. Then you have the fact that they both overlap in places. I see them coming together."

"Conventional science is dominant now, but the new psychic science has already begun. It will bring great changes over the next

91

200 years because man's whole concept of the universe will be different. People will really be able to use their minds within more balanced states of Self-Conscious-Awareness. The emotionality and corruption of religion and science will end and this new spiritual science will take its place."

"Right now we are at somewhat of an impasse. We don't have the formulae that will accurately predict psychic phenomena. The one good example I use is experiments with telepathy between identical twins. They had senders and receivers. They found that a very high and significant percentage could send and receive symbols and ideas. But what they also found out is that the receivers got some messages six months before the experiment was ever done! Not only that, they got them up to six months after the experiment was over too. You see how this can present a challenge to creating a formula?"

"I can tell you this: many great beings lived here in the past. They went way beyond Einstein and the others in their science. In the future they will discover just how many there were and what they knew."

His trend of thought immediately returned to the basics.

"The importance of using abstract symbols in math is that it allows you to by-pass limiting emotional patterns. These are the patterns that program your actions. They make you predictable and therefore controllable. Of course, breathing Kriya also counter-acts this problem".

"The most ancient symbols that came down to us are four in number. They are a function of four that equals the One, or God. The symbols are the circle with a dot in the center, the plus sign or cross (+), a large curved comma sign or Moon like crescent, and a circle without the dot (O), or sometimes the asterisk/sextile glyph, which is a plus sign with two more angular lines (*). The Hebrews also said they were four, which in one expression is their IHVH."

"You remember that I said that God was a circumference whose center is everywhere. Well, that's the circle with the dot in the center, and, as you know, it is also the symbol for the Sun. The circle has a circumference that is 360 degrees. One revolution around this circle is, and only can be, equal to 2pi radians. Keep these symbols and facts in mind."

As usual, I was completely overwhelmed and confused. Shelly then went on to explain to me that what he was about to reveal were his most abstract concepts. I have come to think of it as his outline of a thesis on mystical science.

"There are two basic kinds of existence. Finite existence: this has a beginning and an end. It is limited within time, like the meaning of Saturn. Therefore it is imperfect, flawed, bound and restricted.

The other kind of existence is Transfinite, it has no beginning or end and it is unrestricted, and limitless in its nature.

Let's look at a triangle. It has three sides, angles and points. The sum of the interior angles is 180 degrees, but the sum of the exterior angles is 900 degrees. The important idea about this is that it divides space into two parts. The interior is finite and bound. The exterior is transfinite and unbound. When we consider all of the 33 factors about a triangle we realize that it is all of these at once. The oneness is the same as when the three factors merge in perfect meditation equaling the fourth factor, which is more then the sum of its parts.

Science knows quite a bit about finite existence, but when it comes to transfinite existence it knows very little. They have a small idea about it in three or four ways. The first is the infinity of numbers, counting from 1 to infinity. The second is that the number of points on a line are more then there are numbers to count them. The third is that the curves or curved lines in space are greater then the first two. Then there are a whole bunch of theories that have not been proven yet.

The first letter of the Hebrew alphabet is Aleph, so we count Aleph/One, Two and Three. We are stuck with this primitive counting system of three, like someone who is mentally deficient and unable to count higher then three. I like to think that the Aleph/ Four is the memory track of Transfinite Beings, the self-existing ones. It has a greater infinity then the first three. Now you know where real memory may exist, and it is far beyond the humanoid form.

There is an Aleph-to-Aleph par, but we are not really sure what it is. We do know that God is transfinite, because when you have Aleph-to-Aleph par and compare it to the first infinity of numbers, it makes that seem very finite. Somewhat like a limited point out of which the dimensions manifest, relatively speaking. Yet, this par factor, in it's own existence, is infinite and unbound."

Answering the question that I didn't ask, he was moving right along.

"Then how do we actually express the way the finite existence comes out of transfinite existence? You see the infinite amount of numbers in transfinite existence is the lower common denominator that can be used to measure everything. The infinite amount of points on a line are the units, or numbers, showing the amount of Self-Existing Ones that there are."

"When the SCA (Self Conscious Awareness) of any being begins to wake up, there is a dimensional movement. To tell you the truth, this point, which is your essence, created all the dimensions, so to it there are none new to discover. Remember, Euclid defined a point as a dimensionless existence."

"As it (SCA) moves, the first dimension it creates is linear space unto itself. Then it begins to move at right angles to itself creating a plane. When it moves at right angles to that plane a cube is created. The next movement creates time as it is inside the finite triangulations. This means we are a +1 and one dimension removed (-Xsq.) from our Self."

"The formula for the dimensional movements starts out with the interplay between the real Self and the not Self, or -X times +X which equals -Xsq. Then when we factor it -X times -1, then Xsq. times -1, and the square root = -Xsq. But then you can't use the sq. root of -Xsq., or even the Sq. root of -X; it's impossible unless there is a 90-degree dimensional movement."

"Now those straight lines in space that I mentioned, they are male in their nature. They don't communicate with each other. The curved lines in space are feminine in nature. They are in telepathic communication with each other.

"Gravity causes these curved lines in space, because it tells space how to curve, and it always seems to curve back in on itself. Then the curvature tells matter how to move. This is an old statement. Gravity comes the closest to describing this third infinity. Yet it does not, necessarily, have gravity waves."

"The curvature of space is the result of a time phase relationship. It is similar to the many individual paths that lead to God Consciousness, or in this case, Aleph-to-Aleph par. It is so great, vast, and infinite that it is incomprehensible. Even the last Buddha did not, and could not, really speak about it because it was so totally unbound."

"We know that Einstein and others knew about all the kinds of relationships between: time, space, motion, matter, energy and light. People believed him like he was a Pope or a King; there are a number of unanswered paradoxes in his theories."

"The classic theory was where the person on the train shoots an arrow at 100 M.P.H., while the train is moving at 100 mph, so the arrow has to be moving at 200 mph. Yet the outside observer still sees the arrow moving at 100 mph. When the train and the arrow are going in opposite directions, then the outside observer sees the arrow drop to the ground. The man on the train, however, sees the arrow moving at 100 mph. Both are true according to the law of relativity. Think about this, if you were moving at 200 M.P.H. then you could walk on water, because at that speed water acts like a solid!

"When we consider the speed of light, it didn't obey the above laws either. From our place in the universe it appeared to move at a constant of 186,000 miles per second. But when we observe light in the most distant areas of the Quasars, it appears to move at ten times the above speed. When light moves at these tremendous speeds, time does not exist.

"Some Russian scientists feel that time is an energy field where all events happen simultaneously."

"In the energy field of time there is a clockwise and counter clock rotation. When this field weakens, it does so more slowly then does the quicker weakening gravity field. So time is variable and light has certain levels of absoluteness, and gravity is just a strange force that we don't fully understand yet."

"Man has created a multitude of things in time and within dimensions. Therefore he must have existed before time."

"It should take no time at all to get to the Quasars. The curvature of space in a Quasar has so much energy in a cubic foot of space; that any atom will glow. The way that light bends shows that space is both linear and non-linear. So energy and time are different there, it should take no time at all when you travel through time to get there."

"But back within finite existence, for example; there are certainly differences in the amount of time it takes any being to become Self Realized. This is also partly because of the curves in space within transfinite existence."

"Einstein would not go along with the rest of the scientific community about the quantification of gravity. According to him gravity was nothing more then curved space. When gravity is quantified you have a graviton, which has a spin and everything. If it is real then we have to have an anti-graviton. This could take you up in the air like a balloon because it's anti-gravity. Einstein's theory is wrong in this respect, this much I know. Why? Because saints float! Something has to be wrong with the way the gravity force field is presently understood, because in deep meditation it's possible to bend space in the opposite direction."

"My formula says that the only difference between energy and mass is that they are the reciprocal of time and space. S over $T = E$ and T over $S = M$."

He stopped speaking momentarily while his face developed a flushed smile.

"The other day I was going through the T.V. channels and I heard someone playing a guitar and singing to God. He says to God; "How long is a million years to you, God? God answers and says, just a second." Then he says; "How much is a million dollars to you God? God again answers and says, "It is just a penny." Then the guy says, "God will you give me a penny?" God answers and says, "Yes, I will, in a second!""

His statement hit me in a profound way, so I didn't laugh. He sat quietly for about a minute. As usual I began to hear his voice before he started speaking again.

"You know a lot of our problems come from the fact that we are out of context with time. It says in the Bible that a thousand years of man is equal to one year of God. So time is relative to your state of awareness. We are more affected by time due to our states of imbalanced SCA. Like when you want something in a dream, it doesn't happen then, there is a time delay. In your own subjective time, it's manifest, but not in the everyday world."

"One of the properties of the soul is that any change in Self-Conscious Awareness will cause a change in space, too. It's the signature of the mentor, so to speak."

"In a very abstract and symbolic way, the curves in space are similar to the photons within electromagnetic theory. Photons can communicate through the many electro-magnetic existences."

"Even when they take matter and anti-matter and run them toward each other in a cyclotron, it's still a finite experiment. The most unimaginable concepts are found in the transfinite existence."

"This is why we have go to back to the laws of Self-Conscious-Awareness. When you apply these laws to the solar system you get Astrology. Astrology is a simple analogy but highly contaminated. SCA applied to the palm is chiromancy, applied to the Kabala it is numbers; to the spine, it's breathing Kriya."

"It's actually a combination of the laws of SCA, moral codes and the various paths that lead to God Consciousness. The basis for all the moral codes is variations in the states of SCA. They produce curved telepathic waves."

I then needed to pose a question, "Shelly, how do we really know we know something, or anything for sure?"

"It's difficult. First of all it's like you have two computers inside your head. One is analog, the other digital. The analog is the intuitive feeling part; it has a vision of the whole system. Digital is the rational part that breaks things down into alphabets and math. You, as the Higher Self, are the observer of both. Remember, I told you that you are dimensionally removed from things, because you are really no-thing."

"Now, when you do any kind of probing, your preconceived ideas and your emotional content will cause you to be biased. When you have some knowledge, it curves space so you can't see things in a clear way. It really depends on your position (SCA), the "type" of knowledge that you have, and how truthful you can be about anything. Even the truth is relative, and as for absolutes, we used to think the speed of light was absolute, but look how that's changed."

"I do know that any energy created is stronger within the sender then with the receiver. So anything you are aware of produces a signature, and is stronger in the person who creates it. So be careful what you create."

"Whatever you are aware of lights up your spine in a different way. If you thinking of a pear, then you start thinking of a peach, the light will be a little different.

Whatever you create in yourself is a seed that has to be reaped somehow. There is no supreme being in a court that is judging you. You are the one that judges yourself by your thoughts and actions within various states of SCA. This is true for all beings that have SCA, and not all do. These ideas are of greatest concern to the SCA of transfinite Self-existing ones.

"In deep space there are only two kinds of lines: the straight and the curved. However, within a gravity field where there is a reference point, we have four basic lines, keeping in mind that energy is also matter (E=MCsq.). These lines are described as the cool blue vertical line. It is austere, commanding, regal, digital, and like the Sun. Then there is the soft green horizontal line. It is retiring, restful, peaceful, sleepy, analog and can mean death. It is like the Moon. Then there is the angular red line. It implies action and energy. The last one is the curved rainbow colored modulating line. It means beauty, and it is a form of gravity, and in this case finite. None of these lines are parallel to each other, meaning we can have real perspective."

"Now in the higher dimensions of deep space, the curved and straight lines can refer to the meaning of transfinite existence. Symbolically, the straight is the number one, and the curved line in its more perfect form is a zero. This is the number ten (10). They naturally move toward each other and eventually they approach the speed of light. The straight line and the diameter of the circle become smaller and smaller. But when they meet they can't pass through each other. So now we are back to the infinite number of points, and the one point. The ancients said that: God is a circumference that created a center. This center point is everywhere. Why? Because whatever point in space you occupy, the Quasars are always about 16 billion light years away." So space has to be an extended curve and circle.

"The point and the center can be very descriptive of the repeating "four-dimensional unit of existence," and maybe beyond."

"So lets look again within the microcosm and the macrocosm. We have the four ancient symbols I mentioned earlier. They represent the various types of Self Conscious Awareness. This is the paradox of the two infinities, and it is the best way to express the Cosmic Dreamer. These symbols are used to express conditions in time and space as well as beyond time and space."

"Now, lets go back to the other curved lines to see how they work. They are a form of psychic communication or telepathy. The way they can be measured is by observing electro-magnetic waves traveling through space. Lets say they travel at 300 million meters per second. Then it's velocity over one second (V/1). If the vibrations are 30 million per second, then that divided by 300 million, gives us 10 meters as the length of each wave.

"I told you about the telepathy between identical twins. Well, they also found that distance had no effect, whether it was 30 feet or 3000 miles. Yes, there are wave/curved lines involved in telepathy but what kind of wave is it?"

"I also told you about the different Aleph infinities. The infinite number of points on a line represents the Self-existing ones. They, in turn, can use the even more infinite curved lines to communicate throughout all existence. The straight lines in space are completely linear in its deeper meaning. They are male-like and can occupy the same position in space without interfering with each another."

"Since we are really beyond beginnings and endings, we can have many types of dimensional movements. The impossible becomes possible and anything can take place. We may wonder what reality is any more. Well, reality is what you are relative to. If you see big pink elephants coming toward you, "You had better run."

"Almost anything you can conceive of, or that you ever have imagined, can have existence. The only limit is the degree of your creative abilities. God is a Self-existing one and he created a whole cosmos. So why couldn't any other SEO's create anything they want. If their creation is not mathematically feasible, then it won't have balance and it will fall to pieces."

"I mentioned that a four dimensional unit repeats itself. You see, we are back to the four again. The first dimension is the square root of minus one. The second is the square root of minus 1, times itself, which is minus one. The third is the square root of minus one times itself, and then that answer times itself, which is minus the square root of minus one. The fourth is the same as the above, but with one more multiplication of the same, which is plus one! This then repeats to the twelve par. So, plus one is not so simple. It took a four dimensional unit to make it."

"Even though we have the +1 individually, it is still one dimension removed from the Self, which is the -Xsq. This came about with the paradoxical equation (shown earlier) between the Self and the not-Self."

"The four ancient symbols, or stages in meditation, relate to all this. It's all a formula of how existence works. Showing the interactions leading to the "fourth" is always an event within the memory track of all who have true Self-Conscious Awareness. The physical component of these memories is partly stored all over the body in the light/ weight RNA molecule."

"Who is the viewer of the event and who is the viewed? It's the Self that is viewing the not Self, which creates an uncertainty principle and an energy differential which can curve space to its maximum by making a circle."

"Let me try and put it together now."

Confused and somewhat numb, I think I mumbled something like, "Oh God".

"In reality everything relates to the circle and the relationship of the diameter and radius to the circumference. The Radian is a pure cosmic measurement we get by the formula: angle equals arc divided by radians. All angular degrees within a circle can then be understood. Most importantly, is that infinite pi is expressed by the "circle" with the point in the center or the "asterisk.""

"The nice thing about it is that one revolution can only be equal to 2pi radians. If pi (3.14) varies so does the radians per circle. So 2piR equals 360 degrees and 1piR equals 180 degrees."

"When pi equals 2 then we have 4 radians. There are never less then 4 radians or more then 6.28 in a circumference. The 4 radians is the smallest anything can become, therefore it represents the finite microcosm and is connected to the plus or the cross symbol. It is the smallest, because when pi equals two, it means that the diameter is one half of the circumference. This maximum curvature can explode in a big bang."

"There is a very old creation story called the "Law of the Mists." It comes from an ancient land of Sumer in the Mid-East. They said there was a large female dragon that lived in a sea of chaos where light did not exist. She had a life and death hold over all beings. Then, all the beings decided to revolt against her control. They scattered her infinite parts throughout the cosmos. She then became the light, stars and the planets."

"So, you see that the female is mother of the creation cycle. In fact, because curves can't occupy the same position of space, this allows beings to become aware of each other. Within this exclusive principle there is energy and gravity."

"Then it follows that the 3 lines that makes the 6 points of the asterisk/sextile and/or the circle "with" the center point are the symbols for transfinite reality."

"The "Moon/crescent," or comma symbolizes the variations of pi. I told you that the Father Creator was beget by the Mother. This is naturally a paradoxical expression that does not limit the seemingly impossible concept of the double Godhead."

"When you combine these symbols you can show how the planets express the variations of the divinity. The Venus glyph has the circle over the cross/plus; this then is God over matter. But with Mars you have almost the opposite, because the stylized plus (pointer) is somewhat over the circle. Mercury is the crescent or variations of pi over God the circle, which is over matter. Remember these are symbols for love, human actions and the mind, respectively.

"So the four symbols express the laws of nature using the variations of pi. Two pi (2pi) radians are equal 360 degrees. Because 2 times the radius is equal to the diameter, right? Now, if we divide pi by 6 that equals 30 degrees, or 1/12 of the circle, which is the amount of degrees in a zodiacal sign. Now you can show the angular relationships between planets and points used in Astronomy and Astrology. 1Pi over six is 30 degree Mercury type aspect, 12X30=

360. 2pi over 6 is the 60 degree Venus aspect. So then 3pi over 6 is Mars (90), 4pi over 6 is Jupiter (120) and Saturn is 4pi over 6 (150). Then the Moon is 6pi over 6, and the Sun is 12pi over 6. Each variation of pi increases by a factor of one."

"Now you have the two lights and the five ancient planets, go ahead and add them up, 1+2+3+4+5+6+12=33. You see it's thirty-three (33); this goes right to the basics of occult math. There are 33 vertebrae in the spine connected to 6 centers, which in turn are activated by 12 sounds. Also remember the twelve houses in a person's natal chart are really the six spinal centers. Remember, I showed you the twelve phases or steps in SCA starting with the first of the zodiacal signs (See Next Chapter). It's an old pattern where ideas and symbols are arranged in sequenced order just like in math. You can also see this very clearly in the Kabbala of numbers and the magical squares of the planets."

"These formulae apply anywhere in existence whether it is in or out of God's Cosmic Dream! At some point any being with increased SCA will realize these same laws."

"All of these basic laws that I have been talking about lead to other important laws of existence. The sequence of the basic laws remains important. If you can add, subtract, multiply and divide you can understand quite a bit. Eventually it does get to calculus, imaginaries and beyond."

"Remember, God is transfinite, but his creation, or dream, is finite. He has dreamt other dreams before this one. There are also other Cosmic Dreamers beyond this dream that we are presently in."

"I have collected a lot of information, and I have tried to simplify it by using various symbols. In the process they may reach the level of abstractness where no one can follow my thinking process any more."

"One of my new formulas says; A3=sq.root of * times +. Aleph/Three (the amount of curved lines in space) is equal to the square root of transfinite reality/God (the asterisk/sextile or circle with the dot in the center), times the cross, a form of matter."

"Shelly, now all you have to do is figure out what it all means!"

"Yes, I did figure out where the (susamonic) balanced state is at."

"What position is that, Shelly?"

"If I can figure out the mathematical meaning of the "cross" and the "sextile" in this formula, then I can express the balance state, because it is between the two! The key to translating the formula for God is the understanding of how the basic four symbols create all the symbols for planets, and the other bodies and energies throughout the cosmos.

"In the space of transfinite existence there is room for everything and every experience. Basically, it comes down to five areas: Positive and negative space along with linear, non-linear and dimensional space. Remember that energy is also matter ($E=MC^2$.). So, beings, energy, and objects can occupy the same position in space because they are dimensionally removed from each other and at different frequencies."

"There is just as much negative existence as there is positive in existence. The negative is the difference between the circumference and where the diameter used to be. That's where we find the point of SCA. When the diameter is more then circumference, we have positive space. This is why time is positive and expansive in the astral worlds, but it's negative here in the waking world. There are always inversions that take place. The astral worlds are in the center of the atom (Sun), not in its perimeter."

"Let's go into the eleven dimensions that science presently is focused on. They think there are ten that are of space, and one of time, I am not sure they are right. I think there is one more of time or none at all. Now this is all pure conjecture again. Let's say you have a dimensional plane, which has length and width, but without thickness. If I roll it up, it can be rolled to infinity without thickness. I can roll the plane into a line by its width, then I can roll the line to a point, and this space is then all rolled up. This is what happens to all the rest of the dimensions above the basic first three (units).

Another possibility is that the basic "four dimensional unit" may repeat or rotate four times, giving us 16 dimensions. Of course, each four dimensional unit tries to maintain a contained non-singularity. In a manner of speaking, it's at war with singularity. The old interplay between light and darkness. God is the all, and therefore singularity is like the Devil, the individually of a multi-dimensional non-singularity."

103

"Now, sometimes I have said there are 17 dimensions because I found an energy differential between the first and second units of four. There seemed to be a greater torque or twist. I have seen this electro-chemical, dimensional leakage with coils and condensers in electronics. I think a type of energy was flowing like pranic/lifetrons but I had no way of measuring it. Somehow, it was causing the right angle rotations between dimensions effected by the gravity mass.

"For example, Jupiter is giving off more energy then it is absorbing."

"Now I have also seen energy flows in electronics without gravity fields, so something is wrong. There is a fifth major force field that is some form of psychic energy. It seems to be the variable left over in gravity experiments.

But Shelly, didn't you say it was natural for the individual SCA to create realities?

"Yes, that is right, but God is balanced SCA, a very important point. He is the point singularity. As it breathes out the universe comes into existence, and when he breathes in, it is dissolved. Every time he does this for a number of times, he will create a very balanced, steady state universe that won't have to be destroyed."

Shelly went over to the bookshelf. He knew exactly where a certain book was located in spite of his blindness. He handed it to me and asked me to read from the first two chapters.

"Formless and Void... Is that the part?

He whispered, "Yes."

"It says, "The Book of Concealed Mysteries" and the "Book of Equilibrium of Balance".

"That's the purpose of existence", he remarked.

"For before countenance beheld not countenance... this is part of your poem", I added. "The Kings of ancient times were dead and their crowns were found no more and the earth was desolate..."

With a mildly stern look he replied.

"In other words, a being can create a cosmos, but sometimes it can't keep it in balance. The Kings are personified force fields. They could not maintain the force field of their creation, and therefore they were destroyed by their own imbalanced forces."

"Always remember, this Cosmic Dreamer opened up his cosmos for us to come in and learn his techniques. Through unselfish love we learn to obtain balanced Self-Conscious Awareness. We can tear the fabric of his dream, but in the process he is still nourished by our memory tracks. He also feeds you through the medulla Moon center at the back of your head, called the "Door of God."

"Each person has free will and they can do as they see fit. When they do this, it's usually at the expense of others and then some conflict ensues.

Within the vastness of this dream it is easy to get lost. We need to know where we are and where we are going. I am aware that I am. They are another eleven twelfths of variations of the "I am" awareness. Basically then we only know one twelfth of what is possible. We have to solve the rest of the maze to escape from animal consciousness."

"This is why the ancients always said, Man know thyself, for this is the foundation of all wisdom. The mystery of existence is revealed by knowing thy self"

"Love is like pi—natural, irrational, and very important."
—Lisa Hoffman

"The generation of random numbers is too important to be left to chance."
—Robert Coveyou

"God doesn't play dice with the Universe."
—Elbert Einstein

CHAPTER 9.

THE MAGICAL REALITY OF LIFE

During the course of my visits, Shelly alluded to the fact that there were certain laws of nature little known by modern science. He explained that a precise system of correspondences, and the procedures to implement forces, had been passed down through the centuries.

He also said there were two valid ways of viewing life, one was the literal way, and the other was by symbolic association. The latter was the occult method, a rare choice, and one not always immediately accessible.

"Shelly, you have made certain statements about magic and it's possible uses, I wonder if I could ask you some questions in this area?"

In a deliberately slow manner he responded with a clear, drawn out, "Yes".

"Before we talk about magic, let me point out the ultimate magic is in Kriya Yoga meditation. Only in deep meditation are we free from any and all influences."

"There are basically three types: white, black and gray."

"White magic intends to work with the forces of nature in a sympathetic relationship. Its primary concern is with helping and healing others."

I pondered to myself. "There is usually a certain amount of immaturity and naiveté' associated with the way it is taught and understood."

"Black magic has another law, that it created; "I sow as I will and I reap as I please." It operates "as if" there is no justice, moral laws, nor code of ethics. It uses the laws of nature as it sees fit."

"Gray magic is a little understood practice that manages the polarities and therefore balances the forces of black and white. It is the highest form of magic and not easily attainable."

I somehow understood that the gray form of magic should not be viewed as half bad. It was half n' half, yet this actually mimicked the universal balance of the two great forces that Shelly had so often described. It was in fact the middle path.

It also became apparent that those who were on the pro God side didn't always give you all the knowledge puzzle pieces. So you came up a little short. Whereas on the dark side they give more then you needed but many of the pieces were false and/or dangerous. Looking at both I summarized, that it was either a case of too little too late or too much of the wrong information too soon.

"All spiritual pathways employ magic in one form or another. Most of the rites and rituals in religion attempt to use magic. Since most of the clergy are ignorant about the symbolic meanings in their ceremonies, they can be easily manipulated."

"On the other hand, the black magicians will tell you that God is pulling a massive fraud on mankind. That he/she is a soul (memory) eater. That "God's will" should not be done only "thy will" should be done."

"Do you see the problems that they both of have? Yet, since all pathways lead to God, they are both being drawn toward the same ultimate destiny."

"Many people pooh-pooh magic, but it is being used continuously all over the place.

Aren't people, places and things constantly trying to influence and control you? Call it what you want, it's different forms of magic, plain and simple."

"If it is this persuasive in society, imagine what is done behind our backs by certain beings that really know the techniques."

"Look, the leaders of this world have sold us out a number of times. For example, in the dark ages a cry went up from the people. They said that they had to work seven days a week and over twelve hours a day just to survive. Sickness was all around and most died before forty years of age. In their hearts and minds they begged for help. Surely, they said, something could be done, and someone could help improve their lot in life?

"The Kings, the church and military leaders all were in agreement. Through the efforts of the seers of that time, a group of beings were contacted. However, the answer did not come from God, or at least they did not respond to any answers from God. They knew that these beings were devils or demons. Lucifer, Satan and the rest of the infernal princes made promises that they would send help. That from that time forward scientific knowledge would improve everyone's lives. They also promised that the white Aryans would eventually rule the whole world."

"This happened around 1200 A.D. at a French and German border town. All the clergy and leaders of Europe were in attendance. It's likely that they made a solemn oath, which is a magical pact. Then each would swear their allegiance to each other."

I thought, "It is a binding agreement in the more literal sense of the word."

"So Shelly, you are saying they sold us out, to the "father of liars?""

"That is right."

"Well, Shelly can I ask where you got this story?"

"Sure, I got it from a black magician I studied with when I was a teenager."

I got a very creepy feeling, yet I tried not to show it.

"Why did you do this?" I eagerly inquired."

"Why? I was young and he had an awful lot of information. He and his female partner were extremely interesting. Now to what you are getting at, I did not practice black magic with him. We were more friends, then in a student teacher relationship."

"Look, those kind of people simply don't care if the information they give you is a "loaded gun." It's every man for himself, according to his philosophy. Besides, they have to know more so they can be able to defend themselves"

Fishing for a story, I asked, "So what happened Shelly?"

"Well, one time I was over there and he got into a big bragging mood. He told me that he could work magic and force his partner to come to him whenever he willed it to happen. So we agreed on a gentleman's bet."

"He worked his magic, and he told me when she would arrive over at his place. It wasn't long and she showed up. She was incredibly angry, about as angry as a woman could get. She immediately warned him in no uncertain terms, that if he ever did that again she would kill him."

"Some time passed and he told me that to test his power he would summon her again. Then, very soon after that I never saw him again, it was like she promised, and he did in fact, die."

"You see, she was actually his teacher, and I think mostly Native American. She had taught him almost everything she knew."

He certainly had my fullest possible attention now, but I still had uneasy feelings.

"If you know about the "modus operandi" of the other side, you are at a distinct advantage. When you can predict the behavior of a potential adversary you have strategic advantage."

There was no way I could quibble with such practical advice. My uncertain mood was diffused. However, before it dissipated completely, Shelly presented me with an ominous warning.

"You are going to come in contact with some of these dark individuals in your life."

This, I found, was too frightening a prospect at that time for me to ask him anything further on the matter.

"For example, there is a witch that lives down here, I have known her for years. We have always been on friendly terms with each other. She comes around once and a while and we discuss things. She was burned at the stake in her past life. The proof of this is that you can still see the flames in her aura. You don't have to be very psychic to see the flames, either. She is still learning some things about karma. She used magic to kill her father for the insurance money! I warned her about these practices. She acknowledged the fact. She said, "I know that anything I do I will pay a price for it." But when someone does anything against her, she counts her losses, and then she gets out her spell book and goes on with it anyway."

He then continued in his explanations.

"There is a universal law of justice in regards to magical practices. You see, each person judges himself or herself, and they do this alone by themselves. The laws of self-conscious awareness produce a standard. It's the law of karma. I have told you this before; "Whatsoever you do unto another you do to yourself, only in another time and space."

"But Shelly isn't it true that the black magicians don't feel that the laws apply to them."

"Yes, this is true, but sooner or later the forces you set into operation are going to be due and payable."

"Some magicians work a difficult form of magic to alter those future events. When they do this, they add another factor. Then pretty soon they have to do it again. Eventually it gets very, very complex and quite difficult to keep track of all the factors. You can be sure that it will get them in the end."

"Remember, both sides teach the same basic principles, which are neither good nor bad in and of themselves. It's all in how you use the information, as to whether you create good or bad karma for yourself."

"Many in your various spiritual movements want power. They love all the power concepts. They like to feel important and elite. They feel they are doing what is good for the people, even if it is against the will of the people!

"Keep in mind that magic is the art of putting thoughts into action. You need an energy source, and the ability to activate your inner will power. Along these lines, someone could create very adverse things using Kriya if they are not careful."

"With this physical body we are vulnerable so it's vitally important to work above the three lower centers."

"O.K., Shelly how are we to do this?"

"If a person wants to work real magic they have to become celibate for a period of time."

"Shelly, you are not celibate, because you are married," I frankly stated.

"Yes, that's true, but both of my wives knew how to return the psychic energy to protect me. I, of course, could use their psychic force field too"

"You see, it's almost impossible to work magic unless you have a reserve of energy. The woman holds the power, they are the battery, and I told you this."

"The way things are set up; the men have a more difficult time. The pressure builds up and presses against certain nerve endings. Unless he can lift that energy in meditation he is going have to relieve that pressure. When he does this, he dissipates his power and temporarily breaks the loop of energy around him."

Before I could enter some trite statement of defense he completed his trend of thought.

"Even masturbation will temporarily do this."

"As usual, no one's off the hook," I thought.

"You have to have at least thirty days of celibacy to accomplish anything. This time period equals one Zodiacal sign, and sixty days or two signs is that much more powerful, and so on."

"Shelly, I am not sure what you mean by energy loop."

"It is really a dimensional loop which is your personal force field. It makes a circle from your lower centers to the higher ones. The whole aura is an egg-like shape anyway"

"It is only present in Transfinite Self-Existing-Ones (SEO). They are the beings that are capable of performing real magic. They have to have the right knowledge to do this. As you know, Kriya and meditation in general is one of the ways to store the power that is necessary for these actions."

Becoming fascinated by the concept I had to ask another question.

"Could we say that a finite being only has half a loop, because they can't draw the energy over their heads?"

"That is right, they can't make a complete loop."

"When you can lift the energy to the higher centers, you just won't feel the lower centers as much. The physical pressure will not continue to build up. You are closing off the loop so that it does not activate the solar plexus. Lifting the energy is going against the common rotation of the astrological signs, but it is the right way.

"This energy mostly acts as a particle, but when it is a double loop, it acts as a wave as it moves through dimensional space. It takes a degree of Self Conscious Awareness to cause this dimensional movement. It is the observer and the observed merging. So you see,

111

we can be dimensionally separated, not actually, by time or space, but by our own dimensional concepts. You, in fact, are the creator of time and space, and as a result of this at some point you will realize time doesn't exist before you created it. You get trapped in your own creation and caught in your own dreams."

"What are the symbols in our dreams saying? They are personalized force fields that tell a story."

"So you see, we produce all our own limitations. If our awareness focuses on hell, then we are in hell."

"We create thought forms and give them energy and then they can enslave us. Does the man and woman own the new car and dress, or is it the other way around?"

As if to out trump himself, he quickly added, "Boredom is the biggest problem effecting spiritual progress. People will jump out of the frying pan and into the fire to make a change in their lives. We need a change upward, not downward. The Chinese proverb says; "All things come to he who waits". Therefore, know what you want, and when the door opens, and the opportunity presents itself, move in that direction."

"Shelly are there any other big do's and don'ts when setting up your own magic?"

"It's very important that you experience magic for yourself in one form or another. The closer you are to the basic truths, the more powerful your magic will be. There are the magic principles that are universal. Your own symbols are relative. As I mentioned before, one of these symbols is that going up is good and going down is bad. All things that are not really free are falling downward. You have to keep records and do research on your own basic symbolism. You must get as close as you can to the actual interpretation, and not an arbitrary one."

"There are many ceremonies that are only relative. The ones that are absolute are much more powerful. When I say absolute I mean natural. Much of the symbolism out there is just the shaft, so what is associated with them is humbug, and it simply is not true."

"Most magical systems keep people on the wheel because of their basic ignorance about the language of symbols. It's very tricky, all of these various associations. You can move different forces all around, but you are not really neutralizing anything. When you set up a cause, the effect must be a balanced state. Then we are off the wheel and on the stick, the straight and narrow."

"Everyone is born with the same amount of malefic and benefic forces in their horoscopes. The difference is they are arranged in a wide variety of symbolic associations."

"Shelly, there is a difference of opinion between Eastern and Western astrologers about what planets are really malefic and benefic."

"Alright, what do you consider a malefic and a benefic?"

"I'm convinced along with the Germans and Hindus that Neptune is malefic. I think Uranus, depending on the aspects, can also be malefic and the same goes for Pluto. The Hindus go further saying that the Sun, Mercury and Moon can all be malefic, depending on position and aspects. The only ones they consider truly benefic are Jupiter and Venus."

He looked at me with a whimsical stare.

"You know, from this point of view no one stands a chance."

"You asked me what I feel about it. I actually think the planets are a little more benefic then indicated," I replied.

"Let's take the Hebrew/Egyptian system. Venus, Jupiter and the Sun are benefic. Saturn, Mars and the Moon are malefic. Mercury is neutral, it refers to the balanced state."

"But there is a problem with this modern system, because almost all astrologers consider Uranus, Neptune and Pluto malefic. If you just take the six slower moving planets in transit, you haven't got a chance! Man is running down a steep incline to oblivion. There is no balance in this system, like there is with the three, one and three in the ancient system. From a statistical point of view, there is no truth to the modern system, and I would throw it out. Mankind could not survive under such conditions."

"I do subscribe to the theory that Uranus, Neptune and Pluto will become more benefic as mankind becomes more and more stabilized on the spiritual path," I said.

Shelly then started to laugh.

"O.K., but mankind does not have a chance right now with this theory."

113

"Remember, astrology is a twelve system. Like there are twelve ways to write IHVH. Something strange takes place, when you have a perfect meditation, and all equals one. You find out that your wholeness is now more then all of your parts! I didn't say, addition, subtraction or multiplication. I said ALL of your parts. The twelve and four factors are all one. There is also an older sixteen system."

"When you add up the twelve signs, the seven dual natures of the ancient planets and the three mother letters, you get twenty-two. These are the twenty-two letters in the Hebrew alphabet. This is the law of the circle where $7/22 = 3.14$, which is pi."

"SCA functions within this twelve-fold pattern. When an event happens we observe the various relationships of symbols within that pattern. We can then place them in one of the twelve astrological houses/signs and get related information."

"I have tried to tell you that ideas and symbols are arranged in a sequential order, just like in math. Two is one more then one, and one less then three, and so on. We can develop mathematical equations that correspond to certain states of awareness that we are producing."

"In turn, each of the spinal centers vibrates to certain sounds. The arrangement of sounds and symbols is unlimited. That's why you have been given the proven sounds as they have come down through the East Indian Yogic and Egyptian schools. This is a system that allows us to become aware of things that are usually not possible within the scope of our normal everyday lives."

"Meditation, astrology and magic all come together. This is considered the highest form of magic, because of the controlled awareness associated with these practices."

"The houses and signs do have a basic order that relates to states of awareness. I explained to you that the first house was "I am" or "I am aware that I am. It personifies and identifies a person, place, or thing. This is the immortal Spirit."

"The second place, phase or house. It is the soul. All you really possess is a your memory. When changes in your SCA occur, this implies an event has taken place and it is recorded in your memory track or soul." (Taurus)

"Now the spirit is capable of comparing the event with itself, and its soul/memory. This oscillation is the twins of Gemini and the third house."

"These memories become a past record of who we are in the fourth/lunar house. This is the beginning and ending of all states of awareness, (up to that point). (Cancer)

"Out of this reflection of the Self comes a new state of willful and creative Selfhood. The Sun and Moon, and the male and female polarity, see each other within the reflected light." (The fifth stage, Leo)

"Then it is realized that further discriminative details are necessary in the sixth house or Virgo."

"That analysis then weighs and balances the actual differences of the two." (Seventh house and Libra)

"Now it comes into Scorpio the eighth. This is where the discriminative balance is put to the test with large groups of people. This is a new factor and therefore the death of anything unneeded."

"It then expands outward from this new understanding in Sagittarius and the ninth. It opens up into many possible concepts."

"Then the selected preferment's are positioned and organized in the tenth." (Capricorn)

"The understanding or real knowing of all this takes place in the eleventh house." (Aquarius)

"Finally the abstraction of the whole process is in the twelfth. That which is not perceivable in normal existence." (Pisces)

"I showed you how this was done using pi. I am sure mathematicians know about the twelve fold sequential relationships, but they don't know what it represents. Ideas are numbers and there is an order; so one meaning cannot exist except that another meaning exists before it. All the following meanings are then a result of the preceding groups of meanings. Four can't exist without three being in existence in the first place."

"Scientists are coming to the basic realization that all the basic laws of atomic physics and the various forms of matter are meaningless unless somebody can interpret what they mean. The process is intelligent, and it is here for the purpose of learning how to understand it all.

After a short break Shelly continued his treatise on magic.

"Magic can take many twists and turns and it always casts it's shadow some time before the end results. Keep in mind that what you are truly worthy of no man can take from you."

"I then realized that Shelly was saying that a mock event or dress rehearsal usually transpires to give you an idea of what may happen in the future. A magical effect that was set in place in the beginning of the particular process"

"Remember, I told that you should not disturb the dream of another unless they ask in thought or deed. Well, early on in my life, I realized that my thinking and state of awareness could strongly interfere with other peoples mental and emotion states. I learned that I had to be careful how I thought about something or someone. I could even burn out my own nervous system if I wasn't careful."

"You see, you can't "force" anyone to do anything they are not ready to do in the first place."

"With this in mind, I was searching for a basic formula on how or what caused people to have spiritual changes. Around the turn of the century Messier found the secret. The formula said: the effects of what you want in spiritual states and in psychic phenomena were "inversely proportional to your will power". The more will power (force) you put toward a desired end the more it lessened the effects."

"This struck me as very important, and a first step toward a scientific understanding of psychic phenomena". Meditation is an effortless state; you can't demand that it work for you.

"Many times, my strange sense of humor has moved me to work magic."

I knew it was more then his sense of humor that moved him to his many magical accomplishments. He had a profound sense of autonomy and an even keener awareness about personal freedoms. Therefore, he naturally disapproved of how the power brokers and bullies of this world went about their business. It was rare when he commented on such matters. When he did he would keep it to a brief statement like; "What they are doing in that situation is just not right".

In the scheme of things it seemed that a story was percolating. Shelly began to relate a story. Although he didn't say it, I had the idea that it may have come from Yogananda.

"Brahma, Vishnu and Shiva were having a discussion. (The primary Creative, Sustaining, and Dissolving forces in the universe). Brahma said he was the greatest, because he created everything. Then Shiva stated that, "Whatever you create, I can dissolve." Vishnu then stated, "That whatever you, Brahma have created and you, Shiva, have dissolved, it already was within me first." Therefore I am the greatest."

"Then, they all decided to go to sleep and dream about the discussion. As soon as they were all asleep a little blue man appeared. He went right over and began to twist Brahma's ear. "Who dares twist the ear of Brahma and wake him up," he bellowed."

Then Krishna the blue man says to Brahma, "Did you create me?" Brahma searches his extensive memory and answers, "No I didn't."

"Then Krishna goes over and pokes Shiva in the nose and awakens him. He asks Shiva, "Can you destroy me?" Shiva tries to destroy Krishna, but he can't."

"Then Krishna proceeds to kick Vishnu's foot. Vishnu awakens and quick grabs Krishna's foot. As soon as he does this, he has a sudden realization and says, "Oh my Lord Krishna, I hope I didn't hurt your foot?"

"Krishna remembered, the others did not. Each one is a state of awareness; man has these four states of awareness within him. When you are Brahma you are in the awake state. When you are Shiva you are in the sleep/dream state. But when you are Vishnu (conscious deep sleep) and Krishna (Cosmic Consciousness) you are in the balanced states, and you can then remember all things."

Needless to say, the story spoke to me on a number of levels.

"So it all comes down to the state of awareness of the magician. The outcome will always depend on degree of balanced or unbalanced actions."

"There was a time when the corrupt priests of Egypt were asked to find out about all the weaknesses of Moses. After they observed him and checked with their informants, they reported back. They explained to their leaders, that as far they could tell, he had almost every vice known to man. However, they also found out that he could take them or leave them. Therefore there was no way they could ensnare him. He, along with his followers, could then be allowed to leave Egypt."

"You see, he had many vices, but he turned them into virtues, because in the final analysis, he would not let them control him, he controlled them."

"There is one God looking down on us all. We are children of one God. The Sun, the darkness, the winds, are all listening to what we have to say"

The Great Apache Warrior – Geronimo

CHAPTER 10.

OCCULT MYSTERIES

It is in this first section that I would like to pass on some of the interesting stories and strange experiences that Shelly shared with me. The second part covers what Shelly had to say about war in general. It was the ever present "wars in the heavens" that he commented on extensively.

"I have mentioned to you a number of times that there are many obstacles on the spiritual pathway. One of them is gullibility. Because of your chart you, and a number of others are susceptible in that area."

"I'll show you how ridiculous it can get. I had this friend who said that he wanted to come up and visit with me. He said he decided not to, because the energy was off. I asked him how he determined this? Well, he said, "I started watching the stoplights. Five of the seven were red so I took that as an omen and I didn't come." I asked him how many stoplights there are between where he lived and where he worked. He said there were twelve. So I asked him if ten of those turned out to be red, does that mean he would not go to work. He immediately said, "No, no, he would still go to work.""

We both had a brief, quiet laugh at this sad story.

"He overemphasized the symbolism of the event. Some events are just simple events with very little symbolic importance. Every once and a while you get some event in your life that has very great symbolic importance."

"One part of this area that is usually overlooked is with the rulers of countries. What happens to them in their private and public lives can be very symbolic for the whole country."

"I had this one acquaintance who told me that his dreams had some kind of world-wide significances. You could see this gross over-estimation of himself in his astrological chart. He then admitted to me that he had met his equal, but never his superior. He said he would often tire of getting down to the level of people that he considered mere peasants. He said, "They were stupid ignoramuses who had no business being here in the first place."

At this point, I could tell that Shelly was doing all he could to hold back his laughter so that he could finish the story.

"He was quite well known in many circles. Because of his high rank in the military, he sat at the table with Kings and Queens and a number of rulers of countries."

"Well, one time different situations were developing toward major world events so he decided that he was going to tell God personally, how things were not balanced in this world. He then related to me that God had told him that he didn't realize that things were that bad. He said because of his conversation, world conditions would improve."

While not able to contain all his laughter Shelly continued.

"World conditions continued to deteriorate, so I asked him about this fact. He said, "God seemed very intelligent, but since there is no real improvements, I am really getting my suspicions up about how intelligent he really is."

Shelly lost it, convulsing with laughter he tried desperately to speak. When he was like this, the world seemed to stand still; I cherished every moment of it.

"Then we have the temperament of different regions. People are more emotionally expressive as you go toward the Equator. When you move toward the Poles they are less emotionally expressive. It doesn't mean you have more or less emotion; it's just that there is the tendency to express it or not to express it. If the mystic is a Swede, he may interpret emotions as something that can get him into trouble. But, if you are an Italian, emotional expression is quite normal."

"Sometimes people's impressionable natures can have profound consequences. When I was with Yogananda, we had a special place called the "garden". It was on the grounds at Encinitas. It was very well cared for, beautiful and tranquil. Many of us would use this area to pray and meditate. It had the reputation of being a place where some extraordinary experiences happened."

Among our little group there was a disciple of Yogananda's, I'll call him Bill. He had been with Yogananda for a number of years.

One day while he was in the garden, the appearance of Count Saint Germain materialized before him. They had a brief discussion. This disciple then related the story to Yogananda, with a lot of enthusiasm. Yogananda, with a skeptical air said he would meditate on it. The next time this happened, "Sister" was with him. She said she didn't think it was the Count. Yogananda later confirmed this fact. But Bill kept insisting that it was in fact the real Count Saint Germain. He further stated that the supposed Count had offered him a number of material and spiritual gifts, if he would agree to become part of his movement. Yogananda told him directly, that this being was in fact part of the black brotherhood and not the real Count. The third time it happened he was by himself. They worked out a deal and he left the Ashram, never to return. A short time later we heard he had formed a somewhat popular spiritual organization."

"One has to be very cautious in these matters. I was perhaps fortunate, because I was exposed to the supernatural at a very early age. You know that my relatives and neighbors started confessing to me when I was about five. They told me all kinds of things. I can still remember events that happened before I was one, and dreams before I was two. I also saw spirits from a very early age."

"When I was still quite little, there was this witch that used to come into my room fairly often. I was actually still in my crib when it started. Repeatedly, just before Sunrise, she would come from behind a curtain in my room. She never did anything to my body, but she would try and catch my spirit to prevent it from reentering the physical part of me. She tried this many times, and if she had been successful, my body, would have died."

"The first three times this happened I yelled "Mama, Mama, as loud as I could. Of course this also awakened my father. I found out that when I did this, she would immediately go behind the curtain again. Then my father lost his patience, after all, he had to get up and go to work. I repeatedly told them what I was seeing, but they dismissed it as an over-active imagination. I didn't dare yell out loud again."

"The witch came back again, and all I could do was to mentally yell out, "Mama." This made her go behind the curtain as well. It was the only way I could keep her from taking me."

I had to ask. "Shelly, how long did this happen to you?"

"Oh quite some time, a number of years."

"My Aunt and Uncle rented their place from this witch. My Aunt was a real hardheaded woman who didn't believe in such things. When my parents would visit, the men would play cards sometimes till two or three in the morning. One time during the evening, my Aunt went to the bathroom. Before she could pull the light chain, she saw Miss Alpert the witch standing there in front of her. When she turned the light on Miss Alpert was gone. Not believing what she saw, she quickly turned the light off again, and there was Miss Alpert. While she turned the light on again, she said, "that's enough of that, the next time I am going to grab her." But when she turned the light off, Miss Alpert the witch was not there."

"After that she started to get really suspicious. My Uncle Harry was sick and getting sicker all the time."

"It all started one time when my Aunt and Uncle were in bed together. They soon discovered that their cat had been in there with them the entire time. When they looked further, they realized that it had torn up all the sheets. My Uncle got real mad, swearing he then hit the cat on the head saying, "That will take care of you!" As the story goes, a few days later Miss Alpert came over to borrow some sugar. My Aunt and Uncle noticed that she had a bandage on her head. They asked her what had happened. Miss Alpert said, "I missed a step and hit my head on the wall." My Aunt reacted and said, "You are not going to get away with that story, you witch!""

"So this is why my Uncle was getting sick, it was from a curse. My mother then worked some magic that we were all taught, to reverse the curse. It worked."

"My father would say nothing to Miss Alpert."

"Then, the witch put a curse on my Aunt and Uncle's chickens. So my mother worked some magic. I never saw Miss Alpert come from behind the curtain again."

"My Uncle got better, but the chickens kept dying. They sent some of these prize chickens to Buffalo to be examined. They couldn't find why they died. Then my Uncle decided to make peace with Miss Alpert. The chickens stopped dying."

Shelly had a gleeful look on his face, as if to say, "See how these things work."

"One time shortly after my baby sister was born, we had to walk home from my Aunt and Uncle's. There was snow on the ground and it was about two in the morning. For some reason, my father decided not to visit that evening. I was only four then and my mother was really afraid, so I told her I would protect her. No sooner had we started out then a very large dog came close to us. We were a little scared, because we had never seen it before. It seemed that it was guarding us, and it followed us all the way home. After that night we never saw it again."

"Dogs were important in my family. They always came around and howled when someone in the family died. That happened every time except when my mother died, there was no wailing of dogs."

"I grew up around psychic's or sensitives, I know they have marked moods and a irritability that comes and goes. Another problem I've seen in almost all of them, is that it is very easy for them to see the mistakes and problems in other people's lives, but not their own. They have the tendency to live someone else's life for them."

"Anyone who is attempting to grow spiritually, and/or has these talents, has to deal with what I call the astral plane noise levels. It's a consistent background static that tends to confuse communications and experiences from one dimension to another."

"Sometimes it's just not possible to know what type of being a person is in contact with, or for that matter, if it a suppressed part of their own make-up pretending to be a certain entity."

"A simplistic overview is there is basically four worlds; the waking world, the sleep world, the balanced world, and then all of them together which is God consciousness. In Kabalistic language you are now functioning in the world of Assiah. This is everything from here to the Quazars. When you go to sleep tonight you will be in the Yetziratic astral world. Now, in between, or above these, is the Briatic world. It is a balanced, susamonic or shamadhi world. It is also the world of Christ or Krishna consciousness."

"When I go up into this sixth or seventh plane, the beings no longer have humanoid forms. I have tried to talk to them about things of this earth, but they are not interested about what is going on down here."

"There are first, second, and third grades. When you are in the twelfth grade how much do you think about what is going on in the first or second grades?"

"The nicest place for an individual who has really developed their intellect is the fifth plane. There are all kinds of colleges and schools up there. They usually teach out in the open under trees and things of this sort. They also have all kinds of research labs. There are all manner of wonderful things that go on there. In the middle levels of this plane, they don't have to reincarnate anymore"

"Unfortunately, the average American does not go there. They go to a semi-awake and sort a dreamy place. They are pretty much like how they were on earth. Because they are in a semi-dream state you have to talk to them awhile, then they wake up slightly. I call this the higher third plane. You see them resting and tending gardens. The lower part of this plane is dark and dismal; you can hear beings slithering by you."

"Now on the lower fourth plane is where all the heavens and hells exist, mostly based on the various limited religious concepts. In the higher part of this plane everything seems to come together like the focus of a lens. There is a mirrored effect where things cross over and come out again. Sometimes you feel like there could be storms, and that danger is present. But I have only had the feelings; I have never really seen anything."

"Then there is the type of beings that move around there and try and enslave others. They want to make warriors out of them. If anyone is falling under the power of one of those magicians, they can yell for help, and help will come. That is, if they can remember to yell.

"Let me explain. It all depends on your degree of Self-Conscious Awareness where you end up. The more balance you have the greater is your degree of control, and this comes from self-discipline. On the lower planes, they just don't know much, and they follow their instincts completely. As you ascend upward, there is a greater and greater degree of balanced SCA. There is a slight misnomer here, but adequate enough for explanation."

"Shelly, do these planes fit on the "Tree of Life?"

"Yes, there are a variety of symbolic ways that they correspond to the "Tree of Life." The path would be moving in a special reverse order from Saturn to the Moon. The Moon (center) being the actual and symbolic highest state of consciousness."

"Shelly, where would the fifth plane be?'

"It would be the fifth plane from Saturn. So it is: Saturn, Jupiter, Mars, Sun, Venus and the Moon. It is the Venusian plane of unselfish love."

"Then, each plane can have a number of levels within it?

"Yes, like with the Kabala, there are seventy-two states involved in God-Consciousness. (Six planes, times twelve levels, equaling seventy-two). Some authorities say there are seven sheaths. I never have bothered to place my attention on that aspect of it all. What you do notice is when you move beyond the physical. When this is final at death, some people feel a great loss, while others feel a great sigh of relief."

"My first wife Marjorie is in the fifth plane. When she was a young woman she was interested in knowing everything, all the information that there was. She wanted to read every book that was ever written. She had a tremendous curiosity to know. We never had enough books or bookshelves to hold them."

"Right here on earth we have places or nodal points on the grids where there are times warps, and maybe openings to parallel realities. When you look at a river flow it naturally produces eddies. When a three-dimensional being, like earth, is moving through space with tremendous gravity, it will produce whirlpools in time and space. It's similar to the "Devil's Triangle". This stuff is getting way out of control with the evidence showing that there is an increase in this warping out."

"Shelly what do you mean by out of control?"

"You can't always go where you want to go. If you travel on a time and space line you can get out of this dimension. But if you don't turn around and return on that entering line, you get caught with no way to come back! Where you are and "when" you are is an unknown. We know that dimensions get rotated with black and white holes. You could wind up somewhere when it's two seconds before

125

the big bang, or millions of years in the future and any place in the cosmos."

"I told you before that saints are able to float, Jesus was lighter then an equal volume of water etc. This means that gravity can get partly eliminated. Therefore the dimensions get altered."

We were both in a "something to ponder on moment."

"Now, as far as some being wanting to come into this world without reincarnating they can do it. They search around for a healthy body, like feeling the texture of it, and then they kick the other spirit out."

"That would get you into a lot of karmic debt, wouldn't it?"

"It certainly would, but there are some beings that would still do it. Then there are some that would just possess to varying degrees."

"So you see there are all kinds of life forms out there. One of the most intelligent forms of life I encountered on this earth was the spirits of the air. It's a form of life that almost nobody knows anything about."

"Shelly, do you mean air elementals?"

"Not necessarily, it's not an elemental it's an intelligence in addition to them, these beings live in the air. They look like a glowing amoeba, balls of light. I have seen them up close three times. My wife and daughter saw one with me when we lived in a remote part of Minnesota. We watched it for about five or six minutes before it realized we were observing it. It was consistently changing in its form and colors. It's diameter varied from six to ten feet."

"Do you think it was self conscious, Shelly?"

"Yes, yes it really seemed to be. This one was just playing amongst the trees, just like any other life form would do. It liked to play games, but when it saw we were watching, then it became dead still. We could really feel its awareness, as it perceived us, and probed our awareness. Then it gathered itself into a rounder ball, turned off its light, and disappeared out of sight. Another time I saw one, and it was moving very fast. I understood that it was in some kind of an emergency, so it didn't care if it was giving off light. They definitely go out of their way to avoid mankind, they don't like being observed."

"Our general intelligence and state of awareness produces bodies, like we have here, and the technology that we have here. Other physical creatures, like the whales and porpoises, may have a civilization that is higher then ours. But there is no evidence of a technology, at least not as we presently understand it. They speak at a range from 50 to 50,000 cycles per second. We talk to one another at 100 to 3000 cycles per second. By this method you divide 3000 into 50,000 (=16.6), and they could be that much smarter then us."

"These upgraded monkey bodies we have are meant to hold and confine our spirit. It's also very easy to freeze our memory banks this way. The pig is another less desirable option for these purposes."

"I'll tell you a story that may explain some things. There once was a Guru who was a great devotee of God. Yet it was discovered that he had a fatal form of cancer. His students were very concerned about this; they didn't want to lose their teacher. They asked him, "When you are in the high state of samadhi, if you asked God to heal you, would he do it?" The Guru said, "Oh yes, he would." They said. "Then please ask God.""

"I will, I will," said the Guru. Then some time passed and everyone noticed that the cancer was getting worse. His disciples pleaded with, "Why don't you ask God to heal you?"

"I will," said the Guru. Then of course the cancer got so bad, to where he could hardly move. Needless to say the disciples were really scared now. They confronted and begged him to ask. The teacher said, "Let me explain. It is not that easy to do. When I am in that state, any, and all problems in the physical seem not to exist. I am in a deep blissful state, and totally comfortable."

"The next time he went into samadhi he was about to come back out, and he remembered. He said, "Oh by the way, for the sake of my disciples, dear God please heal me." When he came out of meditation his cancer was gone."

"He said, "for their sake," not his sake. This made it an act of unselfish love, he was tuned to the God channel."

"Shelly, so if you were in that high state of balance would you know about the sufferings of others?"

"How can you be aware that another being is suffering when everything is balanced?"

"Having an emotional and psychic panic attack, I asked, "If you are not aware that people are suffering, you won't help them, will you?"

"Shelly in a clear and determined voice said, "This is right."

Now I had to laugh a little as a tension release.

"That's the basis of my question, Shelly"

"Look," he said, in this world there is a lot of suffering, and there could be a big war and millions of people would be dying, right?

Moving his flattened right hand back and forth in a horizontal direction, he continued.

"That's only when you are this way, and in this world"

Then he made up and down motions with his left hand.

"When you are doing it this way, and dimensionally removed, it is not happening."

I wasn't quite satisfied. But, I did somehow realize that beings in that state do not feel the sufferings of others. Yet, they know full well how this physical plane works, and therefore, that suffering is part of it.

It was a different day. I decided to ask Shelly about what I knew was a sensitive subject for him. Another student of Shelly's had told me that he mentioned he had another physical body.

"I don't suppose that you want to talk about this subject very much. It's about the possibility of certain people having another physical body. Do you have another body?"

"It is said that the enlightened Buddha can have a thousand bodies, that he is inhabiting at the same time!"

I understood that this was his polite way of minimizing the importance of this fact.

Then he quickly added, "So what is so unusual about this?"

I felt that he was not comparing himself to the Buddha, but that if he could have a thousand, then surely he could have just one extra of his own.

He further continued the suspected deflection by stating, "Time does not exist like you think that it does. You are viewing it from a physical (pingalic) point of view. In the balanced state (susamona) it's all frozen. There is no motion there, everything is standing still. If you were watching a little girl jump rope and you went into shamadhi she would be a frozen picture in time. A car going down the highway at 90 M.P.H., would be still, everything would be still."

Before I could attempt to ask a clarifying question he continued.

"If you want to be Napoleon in your next incarnation you can be him."

"Shelly, why would I want to be him?"

"I don't know who you would want to be. Your wife could be Cleopatra if she wanted to. If +X exists then -X must also. So you can reincarnate back into the past if you want to."

"What do you think this does to the usual concept of "Free Will", it makes it rather messy, don't you think?"

Some years later Deborah (his second wife) informed me that he did, in fact, have a second physical body. She further related that he was in abstract communication with it. It was in northern China, also male, and close to the same age. That body was of a Taoist hermit. She said that it was deactivated (died) in about 1985. At a later time he revealed to me that he wasn't sure where Deborah would incarnate, so he decided to have a body in the two most likely places.

*　　　*　　　*

Shelly had extensively studied the key concepts within the history of war. He called himself an armchair general and a military strategist. In his usual conversations, many visitors would be inclined to think that warfare, along with sailing, was one of Shelly's hobbies. I knew different. He was a consummate spiritual warrior, and veteran of many battles. Every now and again he would drop a little teaser about his non-physical actions, encounters, and subtle exploits.

"Shelly, as history has pointed out, mankind seems to be in this eternal struggle. In the old days it was about women and property and now days it's about resources and ideology."

"Those things don't have a thing to do with it, only in an indirect way. As I have told you the basis has to do with the "singularity" of God, and the (free will) choices of "individually". The extreme of singularity is a black hole; it is one to the minus forty power. All that has been created by God will return to God, it's the one and the many. You are a distinct drop in the ocean, and various atoms must come together to create an expression of your individuality."

"The wars in the heavens have been going on a long time. The last major war was about 12,500 years ago. It really goes way back to the differences that Lucifer and God had. I already told you the story. You have read the books that give the names of the angels and leaders on both sides, with a breakdown of rank, and the number of beings under each command. There are huge spirit armies that have always been around."

"Shelly you have said that the wars are already taking place in the astral worlds and that eventually it will happen here."

"Yes, in part, and in a number of ways. But there are still certain degrees of intensity. It is going to be enough where an awful lot of human life will be lost."

"By now we were supposed to have learned about the folly of war. But instead it is our main pastime as Aryans down here. You are trying to wake up from an inter-galactic curse, aren't you?"

"Yes," I asserted.

"It's going to take place on the third and forth planes of the astral. Even a little on the fifth. In this type of warfare you can't kill individual beings, you can only limit and enslave them in one form or another. As I have mentioned to you they have put us in animal bodies and frozen our memory tracks. Down here your physical body can be killed. Yet, young men and woman have a hormonally inducted idea that they are actually physically immortal."

I then related a dream I had about being with Shelly in the afterlife. I told him at one point, that I realized that all his students in the dream were not alive in this world anymore.

"So you were dead too," was his comment.

I said, "I never thought about it that way," as we both started laughing.

"You see you think you are invulnerable to being killed. That's what most warriors think."

"Well, doesn't that make me a good warrior?" I questioned.

"Oh sure, in one way it does, you think you are going to make it."

"Shelly, I mean, isn't it a good point until it reaches a certain level of stupidly."

"Yes, because when you are dying you say, "By golly I don't think I am going to make it" He then broke into a deep and hearty laugh.

He had mentioned to me a few times that I was in his army. I really had mixed feelings about what that actually meant. I didn't know if I should be happy about it, serious or both. I simply didn't know much about that area. He rarely commented on what he was really doing. It was somewhat of an off-limits subject. Then out of the blue, he calmly stated.

"I don't play any favorites with any nations on the face of this earth. I don't think that any nation is that much better off then any other."

"Then, from this point of view, you have to beware of misinformation from all sides. Way back in the Roman times they figured it would cost too much to rule the world with an army alone. So they wrote a whole book on propaganda. It was the technique of "rumor," and the spreading of fear. Hitler's cohorts were masters of this technique."

"In the not too distant future, a major important battle is going to take place on this earth and in the astral. The timing of it is everything. If it's the right time for war, only a little incident will set it off. If it is the wrong time, then many major things can happen, but it won't lead to war."

"Yes, Shelly, I acknowledge that fact but I don't have a clear idea who the enemy really is. I mean, how physical are they, or does it depend on certain things?"

"They can assume any physical form that they want to."

"I thought to myself. "This is not what any warrior wants to hear. How can I begin to accept this as the way it is?"

"Shelly, are they more limited when they take on a form?"

"It depends. Almost all are programmed to some degree when they have a physical form. Then there is a whole bunch of them that only have astral forms."

"Shelly, are you saying that you can not always tell the good guys from the bad?"

"Yes". Then he laughed and added, "You can always tell the good guys, they wear white hats."

"Look, if any being tries to subtly or forcefully exert complete control over you, that is an enemy isn't it?"

"Yes, Shelly, it would have to be considered thus."

"Shelly, it seems that the more they try to control us and keep us imprisoned the more we struggle to become free..."

"The more they actually imprison themselves."

"We have all died in wars before, and we have learned the art of war better then just about anything. If mankind didn't like it so much, they would have given it up a long time ago. Remember, unbalance is the norm, balance is a uniqueness in existence."

"So, it is an imbalance to fight against these forces?"

"Absolutely, yet you always have the clear right of "self defense". All this expresses the laws of SCA. You (+X) are standing off and viewing yourself. This becomes the negative as -X."

"No doubt we are awakening, but it is somewhat of a controlled awakening."

"Shelly, it appears then, that the enemy can be anywhere and everywhere."

"Yes."

"When I was a young man, I had an experience along these lines that was almost fatal. I woke in the middle of the night feeling completely drained of energy. I somehow managed to call for help. In a semi-conscious state, I was rushed to the hospital. The staff examined me and found out that I had only a small amount of blood volume left in me. The only other thing they noticed was two puncture wounds on the Jugular Vein of my neck."

"Oh my God Shelly," I muttered.

"They could detect no actual pulse, so thinking I was dead, the Doctor did not order a blood transfusion. After a few more hours, for some reason, he started a transfusion. I can't begin to describe to you the incredibly exhilarating feeling of the blood rushing through my body. It was "as if" life itself was flowing into my being."

"Shelly, I know you must have recovered O.K., but were there any side effects?"

"Just one. For a few years after this experience I had a strange urge. Almost every time I would drive by a cemetery, I wanted to go in there and dig my hands into the soil."

Well I resisted that urge. But I never did find out who or what did that to me."

Needless to say, this story got my maximum attention, it was beyond scary. I really could not bring myself to ask any more questions about it."

We both went into the kitchen in silence, and we each had a glass of juice.

Then he calmly said, "They have a file on you".

All I could manage was a "How?"

"You come here and visit me, don't you? They have had a file on me for years. They first noticed me when I had my ham radio. I was also doing some minor electronic experiments up in Minnesota."

"They think that I am some sort of "sleeper spy". They claim that I am not who I say I am."

I knew that Shelly had a series of twenty-some heart attacks, and then there was the vampire incident. Although I never saw it he did mentioned that he had his own death certificate.

"Periodically they turn their attention toward me. They open most of my mail."

"They do, Shelly?"

"I was sent a letter from Japan, all it said was "Shelly in Minn. It was delivered to me that way. This is their sense of humor. It's their way of saying, "We are still watching you."

His story brought to mind a letter I had once seen on Shelly's dinning room table. In large blue letters it said "Shelly, Florida." It was from somewhere in South America.

"I figure they have a very large file on me by now. One time they picked up a friend of mine and grilled him for about five hours. They never asked me a question. This was during WWII. Just about anybody I wrote to back then, they picked up. I try not to make waves. I don't want to involve other people."

"Shelly, once when I was in my apartment in Boulder, an F.B.I. agent walked right into my room. I was in the middle of meditating. He said he was looking for a person that was in one of my classes."

133

"That's what he told you."

"When you write in, do you think they send you the whole file?"

"I just would like confirmation that I have one."

"You have one, take my word for it. After all, aren't you involved in the occult, what more do you want?"

"Shelly, do you think they are monitoring and recording our conversations?"

"Maybe, they did it for a while."

"Shelly, are you kidding me?"

"No, they could be tapping in right now. When I am here alone I like to give a lot of false information. I just speak out loud and I say just about anything."

"Yogananda had his spies too. I didn't want to disappoint them, so I would leave all kinds of supposed incriminating evidence. I still do this. So I have quite a reputation. Many think that I am completely in league with the devil."

He then broke into uncontrolled laughter. It broke up any tension. I didn't laugh. It seemed that Shelly was laughing for both of us, and any others.

"I look at it this way. If they really wanted to get me, they could have done this already, for a whole bunch of things."

Being concerned I did not ask anything further.

"Well then Shelly, it seems the real bad guys are not physical. So they pull the strings on the cartels and the shadow governments?"

"Yes, basically.

"They have all kinds of information about everyone. It's stored on the largest and the fastest computers in the world. Power like this means we could have the worst form of dictatorship the world has ever seen. I am very concerned about this."

"Steve, let me give you an idea how these types operate. When I was still living in Pennsylvania I was working in a restaurant that was frequented by a number of characters from the Underworld."

"One time I told them that the new political candidate was a handsome young man. I also said, "He was going to get the women's vote and be elected." I told them that it was not going to be good for them. They told me that this person was one of their men. In fact they said, "Both of the candidates were theirs!"

"Another time they asked me to stop over after work. They told me not to come around midnight because the place was going to be raided. So after work I went there, it was about four a.m. The door was wide open."

"The boss then explained to me how it all works, "I pay a group of my boys to get arrested. The police take them to the station and once there they all give aliases for their names. Tomorrow night the same group will be at a different place when it gets raided. This is how they cleaned up gambling in town without really cleaning up anything.""

"He took me into his office and said I could make $200.00 a week. At that time I was making $12.00 per week. He liked me and he trusted me. He wanted me to be his pick-up man for money and fix his electronic pinball machines. He named a good number of businesses he owned."

"But, I didn't trust him. He had taken two of the guys that I went to high school with, and bumped them off. He told me that he was going to do it. I asked him if I could talk to them first. He said, "Sure, but it won't do any good.""

"I told my friends that they were serious. That they were getting somebody from Chicago to bump you guys off. They told me they were only raiding (without notice) the small places that just had pinball machines. Then they both laughed at my warning."

"Then to prove their point, they want right over and raided a big place that had card tables and one-armed-bandits. Three days later they disappeared."

"The hood in charge came into the restaurant and thought it was a big joke. Laughing, they called the police and told them that the two were buried under a big oak tree 25 miles out of town. Then they laughed even harder." I asked them, "Do you mean they are buried there?" They said, "No, no, they aren't buried there".

The police searched and there was a big write-up in the newspaper about it. I asked them, "What really happened to them?" They said that they put them both in an oil barrel and poured cement in, and then they dumped the barrel into Lake Erie." So I said, "Were they alive when you poured the cement in on them?" He said, "Let's just say, by that time they didn't know what was happening to them!"

"I am telling you this story because these are the type of beings that run the United States and the World. They are absolutely ruthless and cruel. They run both political parties. They can change the guy at the top and still be in power."

"The powerful people that run things contacted me one time in the fifties. They wanted me to be their soothsayer. They offered me $100.000 a year and 10% of the "take" which for that part of their operation was two to five million a year."

"They know now that I am not going to go along with them because I have said no to them too many times in the past."

"You see I could be 98% right and only 2% wrong but they would find a way to put the finger on me for being wrong a few times. They said that they wouldn't do that, but I know better."

It seemed like a perpetual field for the power mongering control freaks of the world. He certainly got his point across. Be strong, cautious and ready for just about anything from multi-dimensional beings that would stop at nothing. I remembered the inscription above the Library of Congress, "The Price of Freedom is Eternal Vigilance."

"Shelly, you said it was a controlled awakening. Has it been that way from the beginning of it all?"

"No, but now they are trying to control it more."

"So, they are letting us think we are awakening?"

"We are in fact awakening. The "thought bomb" influences are thinning out, so they are sending in entities to keep us under control."

"Shelly do you mean physical people?"

"Yes, and usually you won't know who they are just by seeing them. They look like ordinary people. Like with this "Ace of Spies" program you were telling me about. The way this guy was manipulating everything, he could have been one of these beings."

"Shelly, I don't know if he was a good guy or a bad guy, he was such a mysterious character."

"Yes, this is always the interesting thing about these people."

"Now, about manipulating and enslaving, aren't you and your wife trying to do this to each other?"

"Well yes, but isn't it a matter of degree...?"

"Ah, now you are speaking, maybe you are becoming a scientist, I'll have to send you back to college again."

If it was a compliment, I didn't let it sink in, because I never knew if he was about to diplomatically lambaste me for something unexpected.

"Margorie and I won a battle in the astral. (1982) We took a point and we could have not taken this point without help."

"Shelly, what do you mean point?"

"A few weeks ago we won a point, we took a position. It was a major point and others came to help us. Now that position is consolidated. It is not the total war it is just one battle. But it was a major victory."

"Why did you have to do it, Shelly?"

"I am at war with the dark empire, I have been so for many years. Why do you think I got pushed into this animal body?"

"Why did you choose that area?"

"That particular area had to be occupied to gain a position of advantage. I am sure they will try and interfere with my progress."

"Shelly, does this mean others can go to this area?"

"Of course, but they have to be in agreement with the laws of balanced SCA. They can come from either side, the White Brotherhood or the Empire."

"Shelly my problem was I was not conscious enough to be there when it happened."

"If I would have needed you, I would have called you. You see, if I start calling you too much you may not be able to get back into your body."

"Shelly I am very attached to my body."

"What, you figure you can always get back into your body? If your silver cord is broken you can't get back in!"

"Oh, well, if the…"

"If that happened, we would have to incarnate you into another body right away."

"Shelly, what would have happened if you lost the battle?"

"Just get ready for another one, heck, I could even lose the point," he said while laughing.

"Shelly from what you are saying it sounds like this is the first time it happened?"

"This is an unusually large point."

"The other beings that helped you, were they mostly disincarnated?"

"Yeah, at the moment they are all real pleased with the position."

"You know that I call myself a magician."

"A gray magician, Shelly?"

"Yes, and I have done some things that I was not supposed to do. If I were a saint I would not have done such things. My humor moves me to do things that are different."

I really had to ask, "What do you want to happen?"

"I want any and all beings to stop experimenting with the earth."

"Shelly, you said one time that it would take sixty billion warriors to accomplish things."

"Yep, but that area is quite a distance from this solar system. Right now the big battlefield will be right here."

"But Shelly, you have said that this earth is insignificant."

"Yes, in the "total" scheme of things, it is insignificant. If the earth were blotted out tomorrow its astral world would still exist. The war would still take place!"

"So, it is going to happen on the earth, above it and all around?"

"Yes, yes it's this whole sector of time and space."

"Remember, most of higher life forms in this solar system are in the astral worlds of the planets."

"You see, the earth is caught in a power play between three different forces, (armies). There are those who are here from outside the Cosmic Dream of God. Those who are from the White Brotherhood of God, and those from the Black Brotherhood. They are all operating on the earth now."

"Both of these black and white forces pretty well balance out each other in strength. They are about equal in force. They have to be, if the universe is going to maintain itself."

"Shelly, shouldn't the ones from the outside be allied with the White Brotherhood?"

"No, not really. It all depends who offers whom, and what they offer. Then will whatever is offered create an opportunity, edge or advantage? This is all still in the developmental stages."

"They each have their particular stories about God and his creation. I have listened to all of them. But I know all pathways eventually lead to God."

"Man has the least amount of knowledge about himself. Therefore any path that opens himself to himself is the path of wisdom."

"Banking establishments are more dangerous then standing armies"

—Thomas Jefferson

"Politician, "An eel in the fundamental mud upon which the superstructure of organized society is reared."

—Ambrose Bierce

"Patriot, "The dupe of the statesman and the tool of conquerors."

—Ambrose Bierce

CHAPTER 11.

DEPARTURE FROM PHYSICALITY

It was the early fall of 1996. In was an in-between time, a time filled with light and shadows.

I had a feeling that something was going on because within the last two years of Shelly's incarnation, I had a number of very strange experiences. In late 1994 I had a high fever that lasted about ten days. It didn't effect my sleeping and eating patterns. There were no painful joints or flu symptoms. I wasn't really tired from it either. The only unusual side effect is that it burnt all the skin off my feet. It was a gradually developing first-degree burn with very little pain and no scarring.

Then in late August of 1996 I was in a beautiful but different place. While in deep meditation I found myself in the middle of a large semi-dark dome. Wherever I looked I saw hundreds of equally spaced white stars. They were all equal in size and brightness. The background was a dark blue. I didn't know what to call it so I started saying to myself that it was, "the sacred vestibule of God". I just stayed there for a small period time and observed. I did not try and explore, or change anything. I did find that I could slowly rotate around 360 degrees, so I did that some of the time.

When I asked Shelly about this he said in a matter-of-fact voice, "You are in the middle of the thousand petal lotus at the top of the head."

I know that I went there over forty times during late summer and early fall. If I had gone through the center zenith star I would have entered God/Cosmic Consciousness. But to be honest, I never thought about it when I was there, nor did I feel any pull to go through.

Although Deborah and I never mentioned it to each other, we both got the idea or message that Shelly would be around till 2004. As we both found out, there was an alternative timetable.

In September while talking to Shelly on the phone he remarked, "The point is, how long is it really necessary for somebody to be here in a body?" I just accepted this, as one of his off the cuff mystical comments, and locked it into memory.

Somewhere during the years of my apprenticeship he mentioned, "Don't bother to come to my death and funeral, what would be the point in doing that." I can only conclude that he felt that those events tended to be very predictable.

Shelly and Deborah had an unusual, but deeply loving relationship. I knew she was very important to him because he told me that he had first seen her spirit form when he was about two years of age. That was about 29 years before her birth.

He was about twenty-three when he met Yogananda. He said that right away Yogananda wanted him to be a celibate monk. Shelly immediately told Yogananda that he knew that he was supposed to be married. He further stated that he had seen his future wives many times in dreams and at times of crisis.

Like most Yogis, they had a lifestyle of high ideas and simple living. Deborah had a very different temperament then Marjorie but her compatibility with Shelly was very obvious and even infectious.

Shelly had had about ten years between marriages with a decidedly strong preference to be in the company of a female counter-part.

Without going into too much unnecessary detail his fatal illnesses lasted about seven weeks. I would have expected him to leave his body much sooner then he did. However, he upheld a deep, and unwritten tradition of mystic's. He literally kept himself connected to his body as long as he could. His reasoning was that unless he did, very few of his disciples would reach Self-Realization. He saw how much karma each of them had, and without his skillful intervention (i.e. burning karma) a number of them could miss liberation.

It was certainly an abstract process where special dispensations are granted. Only a fully liberated being, with a tempered will, and acting with unselfish love could accomplish such a feat.

When his health reached critical point a vote was taken. There were seven that voted. The Cosmic Dreamer, Great Avatar Babaji, Sri Sri Lahiri Mahasay, Sri Yukteswar, Paramahansa Yogananda, Sri

Shellji, and Deborah his wife. It was a vote of four to three vote that Shelly should leave his body.

When he finally left his body for the last time it was because of every major bodily system failing at about the same time.

A few days before he left I was driving through the panhandle of Florida. I was of course thinking about Shelly. I was trying to deal with a certain amount of guilt about not be physically present during his sickness and passing over. Being in my own life crisis was no excuse. Yet some inner part of me did not want to participate in the whole process. I just could not bring myself to see him in such a state. For some unknown reason it was meant to be that way.

As I was ruminating I noticed in my left peripheral vision a larger then normal bird off in the distance. It was headed straight for my truck. As it got closer I slowed down long enough to notice that it was a gray hawk. It flew very low and close in, I could almost hear its talons scrap the roof of the truck.

I was never totally sad after that. Yes, I had many tears and moments of sadness, but the predominating mood was a sober happiness. He was at last free, and now he would be more powerful, creative and influential then ever before.

We are still in a somewhat limited communication with each other. Usually I get brief messages in meditation or in the dream state. Occasionally there is form of communication in the awake state.

In my deepest meditations I am with Shelly and all the masters.

EPILOG

It's not the end of the world, only the end of the world, as we know it! Shelly called it the dawn of the "Aquarian Age." It is also the long waited "Earth Ascension". It's a turning point for all of us.

I remember a story the Shelly told me about Yogananda. He was once approached by a well-to-do woman who indicated that she would like to give Yogananda a gift. When they met in private she showed Yogananda a cashiers check, in his name for $100,000 dollars. She said, "I would like to give this to you as an offering, but there is one stipulation, where ever you go, I go also." Yogananda answered by saying, "Under those conditions I must decline your offer."

As the story goes a few weeks later Yogananda was given a free and clear deed for a number of acres right on the ocean. Later this became the Encinitas Ashram.

Discussing the dynamics of the "Ascension Cycle" was not the original intention of this book. At present I will leave that responsibility to others and to my own future communications.

The following sites have great depth and they are voluminous. In short they are all extremely helpful.

www.goddessatlarge.com – This is the site of Deborah Wisby Trimmer, Shelly's wife.

www.spiritmythos.org – A very special site, with a cognitive and visual approach.

www.cassiopaea.org – An incredible site with great research and scientific insights.

www.trufax.org – Just about everything.

www.earthfiles.com – Real news, that's real interesting.

Also my site www.directkriya.com

Steven Cozzi

APPENDIX A.

Meditation Formula: M=Meditator, O=Object of Meditation and A=Act of Meditation.

$$\frac{\text{MEDITATOR}}{\text{OBJECT \& ACT}} = \text{A PERFECT MEDITATION}$$

$$\frac{M}{O} = A \quad \frac{M}{A} = -O \quad \frac{-O}{M} = A \quad \frac{M}{-O} = A \text{ (not-Self)} \quad \frac{-O \text{ (Self)}}{M} = A$$

$$\frac{M}{O} = \frac{-O}{M} \qquad \frac{M}{M} \frac{-O}{\text{ (M's canceled)}} = A = O = MA = \text{GOD/INFINITY}$$

To be divided into: M sq. = - O sq. Then - O sq. the answer of the dividing with O sq. - to be divided into. This shows a "Dimensional Movement". Then M = O sq. root of - 1

The Usage of Complex Numbers and Imaginaries:

Step 1. Changing Real Entities: a & b to Imaginary Constructs: Z= a + i b, Z= a- i b

i = sq. root of -1 = the sq. root of -1 that is; (i sq. = -1)! Note (-2)sq.= + 4 (+2)sq. = 4

(-1)sq. = + 1   i sq. = -1   A Dimensional Movement. Defining "something" and giving it a minus value when squared.

$$\frac{(i\,b)\mathrm{x}(i\,b)}{b} = i \text{ sq. x } b \text{ sq.} = -4 \quad b \text{ x } b = -4 \quad \text{where } b = 2 \text{ and } b \text{ sq.} = 4$$

b   has no physical counterpart it is simply a mathematical device or short cut

Intermediate Steps:
$(i \text{ x } b) \text{ x } (i \text{ x } b)$ ab

$i \text{ x } i \text{ x } b \text{ x } b$ (a) (b)

i sq. x b sq.   a (b)

i sq. x 4 =   a x b

-1 x 4 = - 4   a b

Z Z = (a + ib) (a - ib) = a sq. - i sq. b sq. [+ i a b - i a b] = a sq. (cancel) = a sq. + b sq.

- i sq. b sq. = a sq. - i sq. b sq. = a sq. - (-1) b sq. = a sq. + b sq. = Real! Step 2.

ABOUT THE AUTHOR

Steve Cozzi was initiated into Kriya Yoga in August of 1968. In March of 1969, he begin to study Yoga in-person with the hidden master Sri Shellji (Shelly Trimmer). Steve started teaching Kriya Yoga and Hatha Yoga in 1971 in Boulder and Denver Colorado. He continues to teach Kriya Yoga to all sincere seekers.

Steve has also been practicing Astrology since 1969. He is one of a small number of nationally certified astrologers by the National Council of Geo-Cosmic Researchers. He is most known for his classic, "Planets in Locality," Llewellyn, 1988 & A.F.A 1998.

Printed in the United States
92905LV00003B/107/A